HOW DEATH SAVED MY LIFE

Overcoming Scleroderma, Lupus & Stage IV-B Hodgkin Lymphoma

Melissa A. Mavour

For more on living and thriving with scleroderma and chronic illness join Melissa on YouTube at the Rainbow in Bloom channel, Instagram @RainbowInBloomVlog or Facebook @RainbowInBloom.

WHY I WROTE THIS BOOK

I have a passion for helping people. I always have. When I was in high school, probably during my junior year, I received a little Thank-You card in the mail. The note written inside was to thank me for helping the person in a way I'd "never know." It was signed "Nikki." The only Nicky I knew would never have sent me anything at all. I asked her, anyway, if she had mailed anything to me and she, of course, said she hadn't.

I'm a Sagittarius. As I recently read about the traits of that sign, I realized I may owe a lot of my character to my zodiac sign. My sign is ruled by Jupiter, the planet of abundance, spirituality, and growth – three things I am passionate about and discuss repeatedly in this book. Sagittarians are also great storytellers, another of my passions. I believe that these innate characteristics are, in part, responsible for how I was able to endure and persevere through the events I document here.

I wrote this book to provide a light of hope for others experiencing similar hardships but who may not naturally have the tenacity that I do, or the belief in themselves that they could, one day, receive a miraculous transformation. I wrote this book to let you know that it is true that all things are possible. And, hopefully, my story will inspire you to find the inner strength to hold on and pull through, with joy and peace.

CONTENTS

And not only this, but [with joy] let us exult in our sufferings and rejoice in our hardships, knowing that hardship (distress, pressure, trouble) produces patient endurance, and endurance, proven character (spiritual maturity); and proven character, hope and confident assurance [of eternal salvation]. Such hope [in God's promises] never disappoints us, because God's love has been abundantly poured out within our hearts through the Holy Spirit who was given to us.
Romans 5:3-5

PRELUDE

Once Upon A Time...

Once upon a time, in the city of Philadelphia, there lived a girl named Melissa. One day, in 1993 perhaps, a day that she could not have known would foreshadow her future, she spoke on the phone with her mother who was at home, about a half hour away, while she was a student at a small Catholic college on the border of Philadelphia County. There was sad news.

"Miss. Lee died."

"Miss. Lee died? How did she die?" She hadn't even known Miss. Lee was sick!

"She was sick."

"Sick with what?"

"I don't know. Something to do with her skin."

"What do you mean?"

"She died from something to do with her skin. Something about her skin."

"*What?* Mommy, how could she die *from her skin*?" Melissa asked incredulously, thinking that this was the most ridiculous thing she ever heard and her mother must be mistaken.

"I don't know, Melissa. He just said it was her skin." *He* being Mr. Lee, Mrs. Lee's husband.

Melissa frowned at the phone, unable to make sense of what she was hearing, and decided to drop it. Maybe she would talk to

Karen, Mrs. Lee's daughter, and ask her what had *really* happened to her mom.

Mrs. Lee and her family were members of the Methodist church in West Philadelphia that Melissa and her mother had attended for years. Mr. and Mrs. Lee were originally from the West Indies, like Melissa's parents. There had always been something very peculiar about Mrs. Lee's appearance; she always looked like she was stiff and in pain. Her mouth was very small and her lips were quite thin and tight-looking, seeming to be pulling inward. Her teeth stuck out a bit, as though her lips were retracted too much to completely cover them. Her skin was an odd blotchy brown color, completely smooth and thin-looking with a little shine – plastic looking – and seemed to be motionless. Neither did Mrs. Lee generally move quickly or freely... But that was just Mrs. Lee, as far as Melissa had known. She'd just had a unique appearance and a distinct way about her. She was such a nice lady, and Melissa and Karen were friends. Mr. and Mrs. Lee had two daughters, in fact, and they lived around the corner, on the street directly behind the church.

The idea of someone dying "from their skin" seemed impossible and annoyingly ridiculous to Melissa at the time. She was about seventeen. How could someone's *skin*, a necessary part of their own body, kill them? It made no sense. Melissa never did get to talk to Karen about her mom, but she carried on with her life, earning a Bachelor's degree in economics and starting her professional life in finance. She didn't (have to) think about Mrs. Lee's illness again for a long time.

About fifteen years later, Mr. Lee came to visit Melissa and her mom at their home, not far from his. He had learned Melissa had been oddly sick. This would be his first time seeing her in several years.

Melissa's sickness had started as a bit of a mystery. She came down with bizarre ailments that affected her appearance and the functioning of her body. One of those ailments was changes to the color and texture of her skin. She had dark brown skin that became covered, in certain locations, by large, scattered patches of white; the patches on her chest had little brown circles in the center. She suffered from exhaustion, joint pain, and stiffness in her muscles. It became exhausting to climb stairs. Normal daily activity, like walking fast and running, became a struggle for some strange reason. After quite a long time visiting doctor after doctor for an explanation, Melissa was finally diagnosed with an illness she had never heard of before: something called 'scleroderma.'

Melissa was in the kitchen with her mom when the doorbell rang. Her mother went to answer it. In walked Mr. Lee. He followed her mother down the narrow hallway that led to the dining room and on into the kitchen. Melissa was still in the kitchen, facing the fridge and holding a carton of juice that she intended to pour a drink from. She looked to her right to face Mr. Lee walking toward her and smiled "hello" to him. Alarm immediately overcame his face as he approached her, greeted her, and asked how she was doing. She responded, "good," but was filled with self-consciousness at the sight of his expression, even feeling exposed as she stood there in her full-length robe. When Mr. Lee stopped directly in front of her, he sharply turned to the fridge and banged it, saying "No! No! No!" Melissa's heart sank, knowing exactly what he was thinking, as though to confirm her worst fears. She stood there speechless, fighting back tears but knowing he meant no harm.

"It's either scleroderma or lupus," he said, as he looked at her.

"It's scleroderma," she and her mother said.

Once again he expressed dread and sorrow. But Melissa turned away to pour her drink. After Mr. Lee left, Melissa's mother hugged her and reassured her saying, "Don't pay attention to him. He doesn't know any better."

He had meant well, but he had gutted her.

Fast forward four years...

Melissa was admitted to the Hospital of the University of Pennsylvania (HUP), where she had previously worked in administration, after finally relenting to her doctor's repeated urging. For about two weeks before that, he would say things like, "Let me know when you're ready" and she would refuse because the thought of being admitted into the hospital, yet again, was unbearable. She wanted to put it off for as long as possible. She knew she was deteriorating and wouldn't last much longer. She wanted to do as much living as she could before giving in. That day of her decision came in March of the year 2012, when she and her mother were at the Philadelphia Flower Show; attending the flower show had become their tradition in the years since it had become necessary for Melissa to move back home. This time, her mother had to push her in the child-sized wheelchair that her uncle had given her. Melissa couldn't get warm, she shivered constantly and she could barely hold up her own body weight, even while seated. She must have been quite the sight, if only for how cold and uncomfortable she must have appeared. People looked with obvious curiosity. While there, Dr. Donald Tsai, her new oncologist, called to discuss her latest lab results, ask how she was doing, and see if she was ready to go to the hospital.

It's a curious thing when a doctor asks a patient how they're feeling when there is a known medical problem. The person who has been making a million mental adjustments a day, both discernable and not, to navigate their reality psychologically and emotionally must stop and make a conscious effort to identify and describe what they are going through. There was even a commercial, run by the Lupus Foundation, that highlighted the results of a study that showed that patients tend to put on a brave face for their doctors. Part of Melissa's survival tactic was to not think about it directly. Even in the state she was in, hanging on by a thread, Melissa found herself struggling to acknowledge and express the truth to Dr. Tsai. His urging to go to the hospital was a bit more stern this time. She still wasn't sure, but assured him that she understood it was important. But, at that moment, it was more important to get through the flower show, which had a Hawaiian theme that year. At that point, Melissa had already been in and out of hospitals for both long and short stays. The longest of them had been about two weeks at a horrid hospital called Hahnemann. But shortly after they got home that afternoon in March, while she was sitting on the couch her mother had bought especially for her, she relented. She told her mother she was ready, and she called Dr. Tsai. He immediately made arrangements to have her admitted. Little did she know it would be nowhere near a two-week stay, and things were going to get *a lot* worse.

Dr. Jason Fritz to the rescue!

Melissa's introduction to Dr. Tsai was precipitated by the quest to find the source of a very severe, relentless cough. Over many weeks the cough worsened to the point that she would cough violently all day long. When the coughing began, she immediately told her doctors about it – her rheumatologist, her family doctor and, later, her pulmonologist, Dr. Jason Fritz. She was bounced back and forth between the rheumy and the lung guy as they tried to agree on the cause of this cough. In retrospect, meeting Dr. Fritz was when the string of miracles began.

Melissa's rheumatologist, supposedly one of the best in the country, had a cute habit of making her wait *hours* before being seen, even if she booked the "first" appointment of the day. When she finally got to see him, there was never any acknowledgment of how late he was, much less an apology for the blatant, callous disrespect. She told him about the cough and he prescribed one of the many medications she had to take, to suppress it. But nothing stopped the cough. He concluded that the coughing was due to scleroderma scarring on her lungs. You see, Melissa had also had

CT scans and x-rays that showed some sort of "plaques" or spots at several places on her lungs. The doctor decided that it was the irritation from these nodules that was causing her cough.

The doctors went back and forth for weeks. There was a lot of wait-and-see; after one medication was prescribed, there was a follow-up to discuss any changes, the dosage was tweaked, the prescription changed and, every time, there was a re-evaluation to figure out if the treatment was working or not. While the quest for an answer was going on, her condition continued to deteriorate. The cough had become a non-stop ordeal, all day long – loud, violent, and painful. Riding in the car to appointments was a horrific experience. There was a peculiar feeling of thousands of ice picks stabbing her in the chest from the inside which hit like an explosion in her chest any time the car hit a bump in the road. She grabbed the sides of the car and tried to lift her body from the seat to diffuse the pain. She had to go through this frequently, with a driver who couldn't quite get the message from every wince, whine, and clench of upholstery. Pleas to avoid potholes and slow down because "it hurts" were ignored. For the month or so before being this admission, the only thing that made the cough subside for a moment was to vomit. Melissa eventually realized, though, that coughing was necessary to be able to breathe, as the cancer nodules took over the air sacks in her lungs. Every inhalation, every exhalation, came with a cough. Vomiting would provide temporary relief from the pressure in her chest and she could catch her breath and breathe more freely. (Years later, when discussing the cough with her family, her nephew admitted, "It was depressing" to listen to. Years after that, even more would come to light).

On one visit, Dr. Fritz mentioned that he had discussed her case with another doctor, Dr. Donald Tsai. Dr. Tsai had reviewed her history and Dr. Fritz's office would refer her to him and make the first appointment.

There was no time to waste. After brief introductions and a review of what he knew about her case as well as hearing her representations of her experience at that moment, Dr. Tsai said, "I think you have Hodgkin's Lymphoma." Melissa had heard of this before, in passing. It's some kind of illness, of course, but she was not sure what exactly it meant for her in those first moments. Dr. Tsai continued to talk about this "cancer," calling it "the 'good' Hodgkin's," and that said he'd like to do a biopsy to confirm his suspicion. It would be done in the hospital and involve major invasive surgery to get a sample of tissue from her lung. That was a lot to unpack. First, the idea of having *cancer*. She really knew nothing about cancer except that, when she was fifteen years old, her uncle's wife, Auntie Sylvanie, had succumbed to breast cancer at a young age. It was something very sad. That happened to other people. Now. How was this even possible?

An immune system cancer in someone with an immune system disorder. Hmmmmm...

In either 2007 or 2008, she began taking a chemotherapy drug called methotrexate. She did not know it was chemotherapy. It was prescribed to try to prevent her immune system from attacking the body it's supposed to protect. Admittedly, she did not take it for that long. Perhaps a year or two. And not consistently, because she was horrible at taking pills, and anyway she didn't have complete faith in the pharmaceuticals since she had already been told there would be no cure. But she had taken it for a while and only now did Melissa find out about a link between methotrexate and several types of cancer, one being Hodgkin lymphoma.

Methotrexate is a "disease-modifying antirheumatic drug" (DMARD) commonly prescribed for the treatment of rheumatoid arthritis.[1] An investigation by the University of Maryland School of Medicine[2] into the link between methotrexate and different types of cancer found that the rate of lymphoma was "exceptionally high, especially Hodgkin disease which had a 12-fold increase in risk" versus the general population.[2] A warning about methotrexate is posted on the U.S. National Library of Medicine website, stating that it "may cause very serious, life-threatening side effects. You should only take methotrexate to treat cancer or certain other conditions that are very severe and that cannot be treated with other medications."[3] She asked Dr. Tsai if methotrexate had given her cancer. He conceded that it was a possibility, but added that there was "no way to know for sure." People come down with Hodgkin lymphoma without having taken the drug or having scleroderma, of course. But the idea that this could be just an unfortunate coincidence was a bit hard for her to believe.

No rest for the weary

For the first two or three weeks at HUP, there was no room for Melissa on the cancer ward, so she was bounced around from one floor to the next, one hospital wing to the other – wherever there was a bed available. On one floor, she had a roommate who had an incessant loud, heavy cough that kept awake at night. The problem with having a critically ill patient on a floor with nurses who are unfamiliar with the particularities of the sickness is a lack of awareness of hazards that exacerbate the condition. For example, the nurses on that floor would make Melissa get up and walk to the bathroom instead of bringing in a portable commode, despite the obvious extreme difficulty she was having breathing and moving. Even the slightest physical activity would cause her to breathe deeper which would trigger her cough. And because she had to urinate frequently, her coughing and the mucus it generated didn't have a chance to subside. The nurses were also very impatient, so she had to force herself to struggle to move faster than she really should have. One of the nurses turned off the suction tube that Melissa used every few minutes to remove excess phlegm and saliva from her mouth, instead of leaving the device on as she was accustomed. Because of the pain and atrophy in her hands and wrists, Melissa was unable to apply the pressure and hand positioning required to move the latch upward on the tube to turn it on. She had the distinct feeling that the nurses were annoyed with her. After two or three days, she was moved to a private room across the hall. But, then, she had to deal with the late night CNA, the young Christina, who probably didn't want to mess her hair up, and walked in – after first responding through the intercom to find out if it was worth the trouble of getting up – with a look of complete resentment whenever Melissa rang the bell for assistance. Christina seemed disgusted by the chunky green refuse that she had to discard and would never bother to properly clean it from the commode.

Of course, a bed eventually became available on the oncology floor. Hopefully, it happened because somebody got to go home.

Ravdin 4th floor

Melissa was very happy to finally go to a floor where she would, presumably, be helped by staff who were more empathetic toward her and her real treatment could get underway. She was in a fast-deteriorating state of emergency. During those weeks, her doctors were busy trying to figure out the best way to treat her; of immediate urgency was getting the surgeon to agree to do the biopsy. Having seen her records – stage IV-B Hodgkin with acute mixed connective tissue disease, asthma, anemia... – the surgeon declined the request because he did not believe she would survive the surgery. That procedure, called a thoracotomy, is basically open lung surgery. It is extremely risky even under far less severe circumstances. Melissa's medical team got second and third opinions from other doctors and she was told, eventually, to build a case with the surgeon. Dr. Tsai gave Melissa updates regularly during his rounds. One day, he came to inform her that the surgeon (who shall remain nameless, bless his heart) was reluctant but said it was up to her. If she was willing to take the chance, he would do the biopsy, presumably against his better judgment. Melissa could see no other option. From her conversations with Dr. Tsai, it was clear to her that the only thing that made sense was to have the biopsy to find a definitive answer from which an informed, accurate treatment plan could be established. Subconsciously she knew there was nothing to lose. If she didn't get treated, she would die anyway.

A year after the storm, Dr. Fritz said during a follow-up visit, "When I met you, you were basically dying."

Safety and security

It was not unusual for nurses to be alarmed at the speed of Melissa's heartbeat. They would ask repeatedly if she was feeling light-headed or dizzy and the answer was always, "no." It didn't *feel* like her heart was racing. Scleroderma causes Pulmonary Arterial Hypertension (PAH), a progressive constriction of the vessels in the lungs that causes the heart to work harder. She also suffered from severe gastroesophageal reflux disease (GERD), common among scleroderma and lupus sufferers as well. She *never* lay down flat. *Never*. Even while sitting up, she felt the sensation of drowning, her chest being engorged by fluid flowing in the wrong direction. It was scary, uncomfortable and perhaps even life-threatening to lay flat. Now a patient at HUP, she was in the care of people who neither seemed to understand what she had to deal with nor asked about her needs and concerns. There was no consideration for how Melissa had to maneuver to manage her symptoms.

One night, Melissa had to go to another part of the hospital for either a test or an observation. There were so many tests... By this time, she knew the drill. She was an enigma and was often objectified. Like the time she had to have a right-heart catheterization for a pericardial effusion at Lankenau Hospital. The resident could hardly contain his excitement at having such a rare opportunity to learn how to perform a heart cath on a real live human being! Melissa laid on the bed, a specimen for the room full of residents who rushed in to witness a procedure they had never expected to see. Gotta love teaching hospitals! The attending physician made sure to get cloths to cover her breasts. The cloths stayed in place *the first time* the resident inserted the long needle thing into her chest at the direction of the attending, who was guided by an x-ray machine to the right of the bed next to her head. (She was not entirely conscious during the procedure because she had consented to a drug to "take the edge off.") But the excited resident didn't quite get the needle/probe in the right location to be able to drain the fluid from around her heart. He had to go in a second time and, in all his exuberance, the cloth covering her right side slid out of place and left her exposed. She tried to get his attention. She tried to bend her elbow to put the cloth back in place herself but the IVs prevented her from bending her elbow. Residents looked away. More entered the room. She told herself they were professional and she wouldn't be ogled. She couldn't get the resident's attention but, at some point, he noticed and replaced it. Having a condition so complex and severe constantly made her vulnerable to being misunderstood, objectified, ignored, doubted, and made to feel unsafe.

Down the line, she would learn the importance of paying attention, no matter how she felt. Healthcare workers, too, are people who can make mistakes, have biases and be negligent like anyone else. On one ER visit, for a breathing problem again, a peculiar thing happened: the nurse came in and asked if she was on any antivirals. Melissa said no. The attending came in and asked the same question. This happened a couple of times and Melissa assumed they were too polite to ask if she had AIDS, because that is the only reason she could think of that they would repeatedly ask such an unrelated question with expressions of contained anxiety. The attending eventually came back confirming her suspicion; he explained that the nurse hadn't read her chart thoroughly and saw something he named, that Melissa didn't bother to remember, in her labs that led the nurse to conclude that she was HIV positive. Apparently "[it] is well documented that the presentation of HIV infection can mimic that of autoimmune phenomena... Antibodies to retroviral proteins have been demonstrated in patients with SLE."[4] So blood test results for autoimmune patients can show some similarities to those of people infected with HIV.

During the months on the cancer ward, Melissa would sometimes lose consciousness but still be awake like a zombie. Once, when a friend came to visit, she felt the dark fog overcoming her mind but couldn't stop it. Another time, her mom curiously asked, "Do you still want to call the police?" She replied, "Call the police? What for?" Her mother informed Melissa that she had told her the day before that somebody hit her in the face and asked if they could "call the police now." Well, she had no idea what her mother was talking about.
"Nobody hit me."
"You told me somebody hit you."
"No, nobody hit me."
But, then, she began to wonder. The thought bounced around in Melissa's mind, as she tried to imagine which one of the nurses would do such a thing and way. Could it be because she couldn't defend herself? She suspected that she would 'blank out' sometimes. She preferred to think that maybe a nurse slapped her to wake her up because she was non-responsive. But that didn't seem like an appropriate thing to do. She never made a complaint. There were other worries, and energy was scarce.

In recent years, the #MeToo movement has forced back memories that Melissa would rather have left buried. So disgusting and utterly infuriating but what she resented more than anything was the feeling of helplessness. There will be no resolution for her. Melissa was sexually assaulted by two doctors.

It is best to only tell you about the second one because the first one, a hematologist (not her oncologist), would make you want to crawl out of your skin. Usually, when the doctor is male, a female nurse must be present. That was the normal protocol when she went to see this doctor. On one visit, he came into the room when her mother went to use the restroom or get breakfast, without the nurse present. Melissa was wearing skinny leopard print jeans with a belt. This doctor once told her she was his "best-dressed patient." Now she thinks maybe she looked too "good." He pressed her abdomen like normal and asked if there was any pain. "No." Out of nowhere, he shoved his hand down her pants as far as he could. A number of thoughts came to her at once. The first instinct was shock. Then, she thought back to previous visits to consider if this was normal. In such a situation there is disbelief and searching one's thoughts on how to react. But it happened so fast that, by the time she could take a breath, he was mumbling something like, "good to see you again" and rushing out the door. Another thing he had never done before. There was no chatting this time. Also, no hand sanitation. He bolted. She laid there for a few moments unable to move, unable to think if she should scream or cry or get angry or what? But eventually, she became absolutely livid. So angry! And there was nothing she could do because of the situation she was in. Her mother returned shortly and Melissa told her what had happened.

The night Melissa "died" at HUP was yet another time she was made to feel unsafe in a hospital. The memory is permanently etched into her memory.

About the night Melissa "Died"

We begin with the fact that she was brought to another part of the hospital from the oncology ward for some sort of test. This was early in her stay after being admitted. She was sitting on the side of the bed, feet hanging and facing the night sky through a big window, in a room directly in front of the nurses' station. Her breathing was very heavy against the fluid in her lungs and, at some point, she became filled with dread at the feeling of another wave of ruthless coughing coming on. She had learned what the different types of coughs felt like when they were coming. But it was always bad. She started coughing very hard and fast. It was that feeling of something being stuck in the chest, forcing a harder, more frequent cough to dislodge it. She had no other choice but to keep coughing, a mixture of necessity and panic.

One of the ways she managed these incidents was to sit up straight because the cough would trigger reflux beside the drowning feeling. When she coughed like this, her heart rate would spike; since she was on a heart monitor due to concern about the speed of her heartbeat, alarms were triggered at the nurses' station. One nurse came in immediately to try to help, but Melissa couldn't talk to communicate what she needed. Alarmed, the nurse tried to get Melissa to lie down. Melissa refused, tightly grabbing the collapsible handle on the side of the bed to keep herself up, barely able to cough out the words, "I have to sit up." Soon, more nurses and doctors rushed in, urging Melissa to lie down. She hoped they would realize that she knew what she was doing. But they pulled her down. Exhausted, she managed to pull herself back up, one more time, despite several arms holding on to her to make her lie down. But she couldn't keep fighting and she couldn't explain what she was doing. So she lay down, terrified that she would never get up again. As she felt the sensation of fluid making its way toward her chest and throat, restricting her breathing, she looked up at the ceiling, at the upper left corner of the room where a round black mirrored object was installed; it looked like the hidden cameras you see at a bank. For some reason, the letter K came to mind. She couldn't figure out why. She thought about what the scene would look like later, when the staff would watch this footage trying to assess what happened to her in the end. She thought nobody would figure out what really happened. They'd just chalk it up to heart failure or something. "*This* is how people die in hospitals. Nobody listens," she thought. Her final thought before passing out was: "So this is how it ends..."

Melissa woke up in her hospital room to the daily morning rotation visit from one of her attending physicians, a young east Indian-American lady who said, "You gave us a scare last night!" Melissa had no idea what she was talking about; she just looked at the doctor expecting her to elaborate. "It looked like a bomb went off next to your heart!" Oooooh! That. Yeah, *thanks a lot.* They must have run an x-ray or CT scan after she was resuscitated.

"We don't know what happened." "I DO! I DO!" Melissa thought. Melissa never explained to her doctors, on any of the occasions that this incident came up, why that had happened. Again – years later, Melissa would learn more. Her mother revealed that she had been informed that Melissa's heart had stopped beating; she flat-lined – *twice* – that night. Also, a doctor had asked if she had "any *other* children." Nice.

This is a story of grace. Transformative grace. Maturing emotionally, spiritually, and psychologically. How I learned to value my intuition and uniqueness; to be confident, grateful, and more compassionate and empathetic.

The title refers to the second chance I have been given due to the "reset button" that resulted from this more-than-ten-year ordeal in my life. Hardships and challenges in life can be the most powerful opportunities for growth and insight, surely. But, while most challenges come from exogenous triggers like finances, relationships and work, the challenges presented by illness are within one's self, inescapable, and compounded when that illness is chronic, disfiguring, painful, and life-threatening. For a person living in a constant personal state of emergency [in my case, mixed connective tissue disease (scleroderma with lupus overlap)], life's psychological, emotional and spiritual issues are heightened in myriad ways. And while lessons learned can be a silver lining to this dark cloud, something even greater is possible – joy.

I shall not die, but live, and declare the works of the Lord.
The Lord hath chastened me sore: but he hath not given me over unto death.
Open the gates of righteousness:
I will go into them, and I will praise the Lord:
This gate of the Lord, into which the righteous shall enter.
I will praise thee: for thou hast heard me, and art my salvation.
Psalms 118:17-21

PART ONE

Vicissitude

CHAPTER ONE

Prelude To A Disaster

Faith

When I envision my early spiritual journey from just before I first noticed a change in my body, I imagine a scene in a movie where I am wandering in a forest, heavy with fog, hearing a voice in the distance but not being able to identify the direction from which it was coming. With every step forward I make sure to look down to avoid any stumbling blocks or sudden craters in my path, keeping my ears open for the direction where the voice would lead me.

I talked with my friends about this feeling of missing something and needing to solidify some direction in my life. They told me about a training called Landmark. They all swore by it enthusiastically. All but one of these women were raised African American and West Indian Christian, while the other was Ethiopian Muslim. They told me how Landmark helped them have more organized thoughts, self-awareness, empathy, and focus. I decided to give it a try. At the time, I had been working an acting job that was paying really well and I decided to invest some of my earnings into this training. The seminal insight I gained was the concept of our "way of being." Our "way of being" refers to the automatic and unconscious behavior and beliefs that shape how we show up in the world. Being "present to your way of being" imparts empathy, accountability, and integrity, as you gain awareness and understanding of your perceptions and emotions and are not ruled by them. This gave context to how I already saw the world while providing a language and practical tools around it. I see it as an extension of what I had been reading in *The 7 Habits of Highly Effective People* not long before. Landmark was a very helpful turning point in my personal growth.

What I also needed was a good church. I wondered if that would be possible in the city of New York. In my conversations on religion and faith with people I knew at the time, everyone seemed to have their own *opinion* about God and religion and fit God into that box. I started attending a church on a friend's recommendation but I didn't like it. Too impersonal. I floated around from one church to another in my Brooklyn neighborhood but couldn't find the right fit. It was hard to find the warmth and openness that I was accustomed to and needed. When I moved back to Philly after my diagnosis, I began attending my mom's church. New Life United Methodist Church was exactly what I was looking for. At the time, I had no idea how pivotal a role New Life and Pastor Evelyn Clark would play in my life in the very near future.

God brought me to a safe place where I would have a foundation, encouragement, and support for the battle ahead of me.

CHAPTER TWO

The Beginning: Becoming A Marathon Woman

Having a severe chronic illness is a never-ending test of perseverance, resilience, emotional fortitude, humility, and patience.

In late 2005, I started to notice that my body felt strange. I felt weighed down and oddly sluggish all the time. Then I started getting heavier, even though my eating habits and activity level had not changed. Over the course of the summer of 2006, my clothes got tighter and the sluggishness developed into true fatigue. My roommate suggested I change my diet; when I told her my diet hadn't changed, she suggested I try working out. Her friend was a soccer coach and personal trainer. She recommended that I let her train me because I was probably just getting out of shape. I was, after all, almost 30 (gasp!). I was used to being naturally athletic and muscular. Previously, I had always been able to pick up where I left off when I started working out again, as though I had never stopped; I was strong. But this time was different. I used to be able to press nearly twice my body weight with my legs. Leg presses were my favorite exercise. This time, I was perplexed at how difficult it was. *Everything* was *extremely* difficult. This was NOT me. It was embarrassing to be so weak. I got fatigued so easily, I could barely lift the amount of weight that had been easy for me not long before. Working out had become a struggle and my body kept expanding. After a few weeks, I decided to stop because it was so difficult to make it through a workout session and things were not improving.

In the fall of 2006, I got a job working background on a show called *Love Monkey*. I was exhausted and feeling out of sorts but I went, ready for a long day on set, potentially at different locations in lower Manhattan, sometimes outside in the cold and rain. I wore a red leather jacket, jeans, and brown UGG clog boots. I was walking around and standing all day with my feet in those wooden shoes, which I thought was the reason my feet began to hurt during the last couple of hours. I was so happy to make it home. When I get home, taking my shoes off is one of my first priorities to get relaxed and comfortable, especially after a long day on my feet. So, it was very frustrating to have such a hard time taking those boots off. For a while, it was literally impossible to get my feet out. So bizarre. I had to sit on the floor to get the leverage to pull hard on the heel while pulling my knee toward me. I twisted my foot from side to side hoping to dislodge it. It took quite a while but, eventually, it worked. What I saw was... Stupefying. So hard to believe that I think I just numbed myself mentally to absorb it. I didn't scream, I didn't cry. I was frozen. I just stared in complete shock. Mortified. My heart sunk. What I saw was my foot and ankle so swollen it looked like a watermelon. I had never seen anything like it. I don't recall pain, just complete and utter dismay. I could only assume that the cause was spending so much time standing in those hard shoes. I assumed it would go down by morning. It didn't.

Pitting edema

I think I had to stay home the next day or two because my feet couldn't fit into any of my shoes. But I had to go out eventually for work. Luckily, I happened to have just bought a pair of Skechers' Mary Janes that closed with crisscross Velcro straps. I could just barely get my feet into the shoes and the straps barely met at the ends of the Velcro. Definitely not a secure fit. Although the swelling did decrease over the next few days, it was still very pronounced. It spread from my feet to my lower legs. My skin stretched so much that my shins shined and if I pressed a finger against my flesh, the indentation remained long after. In researching what this could be, I learned it is called 'pitting edema.' The weight of the excess fluid in my lower limbs was only exacerbating my fatigue and generalized feeling of heaviness.

But I had to go to work. I was working at the Macy's back office by Bryant Park, doing regression analysis. I had told my mom about my feet being swollen and she came to see me one day. I remember her comment, "Your legs are so swollen they're shining." We didn't discuss my problem any further, other than telling her that I felt okay. I didn't know what else to say. My approach was to not stop and think too long about what was happening or how I looked; if I had, I don't think I'd have been able to pick myself up.

Weight a minute!

Over the next few weeks, the swelling decreased in my feet and ankles but the fluid retention spread to the rest of my body – my face, my neck, and my abdomen in particular. It's safe to say the proper terminology for what was happening at that point is 'an inflammatory response.' My body ballooned as I struggled to hang on for dear life to a sense of normalcy, as I walked around like a deer in headlights willing myself not to fall into a state of complete panic.

The (not so) merry-go-round/Getting a diagnosis is murder (on the psyche)

Why aren't physicians more aware of the signs of autoimmune disease?

Of course, I didn't just watch in horror as all hell broke loose with my body. As I told you, it took more than a year to get a diagnosis. A little later I'll tell you how that happened.

I shuffled my exhausted body from one doctor to another, desperately explaining what was happening to me to blank faces on bodies that seemed to be suppressing the urge to throw up their shoulders in an exacerbated shrug. I quickly realized that a lot of doctors do not like mysteries. The numerous physicians I saw seemed to want a clear-cut case that could be solved in a few minutes by writing a prescription and then to move on to the next patient. It seemed that some also *do not* like taking extra effort to investigate further to try to untangle a web of symptoms like mine. This might sound cynical but I have also had amazing doctors throughout this process and I'll always be very grateful. Although initial symptoms can relate to many far less serious illnesses, it seems to me that with autoimmune diseases there are well-documented symptoms that occur together, or in succession, that *should*, in my layman's opinion, lead a doctor to at least attempt to rule it out as a possibility. And although individually these diseases are rare, as a group, autoimmunity is not all that uncommon and seems to be on the rise. But I digress.

Some doctors were blatantly dismissive. For example, Dr. Johnson in Flatbush was not only dismissive but downright contrary. I'm not sure how she was granted a medical license. But only a handful of months after I stopped seeing her, her office apparently closed down before I could get my records. I remember my last visit, speaking to her about my weight gain and the white areas showing up on my skin. She insisted on rejecting everything I told her, even against her own evidence. I said, "I've gained about twenty pounds and I have these light spots showing up on my skin." She said, "Your weight hasn't changed." I replied, "It has actually. My stomach is really big and my clothes are tighter than usual."

"Your weight is the same."

"But your nurse mentioned that I am heavier than last time."

"No your weight is the same."

"Your nurse said I gained 20 pounds."

"No, your weight is the same," in her annoying Jamaican accent. I'm half Jamaican but, at that moment, her parlance was like sandpaper against my existence.

She didn't even bother to look me in the face as she spoke. She spent the whole time typing something into what looked like an iPad. I remember wondering if I should wait for her to be done so we could have a respectful conversation. It felt like she wasn't even listening to me... Until, of course, she denied what I was telling her.

I proceeded to talk to her about the light spots, showing her my knuckles. She told me that happens as you get older. I was twenty-nine. To prove it, she pointed out a couple of small perfectly round white spots on her leg. "See?" she asked. I said, "It's not the same." For starters, the light patches were on all of my knuckles and they didn't have a distinct shape. Neither were they perfectly white like her small, barely visible spots.

Art & life

There is an episode of one of my all-time favorite shows, *The Golden Girls*, that every sufferer of chronic illness who has seen it can relate to. In the two-part opening episode of season five, called *Sick And Tired*, Dorothy is overcome by a profound fatigue that has plagued her for five months. She sees doctor after doctor who all dismiss her claims. Similar to my experience with Dr. Johnson, the first doctor we see in episode one walks into the room and begins talking *at* her, without even bothering to look up from the folder he's holding or even get her name right. After some unrelated banter, she demands he give her his findings. He announces, "Dorothy get dressed. You're fine... We've run every test known to man, they're all normal. You can get dressed, go home, enjoy your life," as though what he can (or canNOT) see in a petri dish is more legitimate than her actual human experience – an experience that she had to, once again, recount to him as if to clear up a misunderstanding on his part about the reality and severity of what she had been going through. Bea Arthur masterfully expressed the emotional toll that weighs down on people in this position, the toll that comes from the frustration of trying to elicit a modicum of empathy from someone who is supposed to be an authority in the business of helping people manage their health. Dorothy then has to face the condescending idea that her symptoms are the manifestation of loneliness, leading her to go further into the symptoms she is experiencing. His response is, "Look, Dorothy, I don't believe you're sick." The upside for Dorothy is that this doctor refers her, although reluctantly, to the neurologist he studied with in New York. Most of us don't get that. Or, as in my case which I mentioned before, it happens (almost) too late. Also mirroring my experience with both my oncologist and initial rheumatologist, the doctor that Dorothy is referred to identifies her problem very quickly and she is, presumably, able to get immediate treatment. Little did I know, watching this in my early teens, when Mrs. Lee was alive, that twenty-odd years later I would be Dorothy.

Having to convince people that something has gone wrong with your body through no fault of your own, that it's not all in your head, increases the loneliness and anxiety that the disease itself can cause as the limitations on your lifestyle and well-being set in. You feel like a fish out of water. The only thing you want is understanding; not to be treated like you're a crazy hypochondriac, exaggerating to get attention, or, God forbid, just lazy. I remember a conversation with a good friend of mine whom I was telling about the infuriating experiences I was having with doctors. I told her, "I'll just have to die and they'll do my autopsy and go, 'Oh wait. That's what it was.' I'll have to die before anybody believes me."

It took my diagnosis, becoming completely disabled, and having to move back in with my mother for someone close to me to stop assuming I was on drugs when, during a visit in 2008, they saw the state I was in. A lesson I have learned about people while navigating life with a chronic illness is that sometimes, when we don't understand what we're seeing, we create a story to make it make sense – a story that often involves making the person wrong.

Getting worse by the day

Pins and needles

I was booked on a "modeling" assignment for an artist that required an outdoor shoot in the bitter cold on the lower east side of Manhattan. It was an unusually cold day for that time of year. I was completely unable to get warm. I'd never felt the cold sink into my bones like that before. And I seemed to be suffering more than anyone else. When the shoot was over, I could barely walk the few steps to the train station due to painful frostbite. I noticed that the undersides of the tips of all of my fingers were black. I held on to the yellow handrail for balance as I descended into the station. It was warm and I was so relieved to get to thaw out finally. When I got home and took off my shoes, yet again I was mortified by the sight of my feet. My toes were completely black, above and under.

Eventually, I would learn about the conditions called peripheral neuropathy and Raynaud's syndrome. Both are forms of vasculitis (blood vessel inflammation), which lead to poor blood circulation as the arteries narrow in response to cold. Neuropathy is the result of nerve damage, wherein the central nervous system cannot send messages to the feet. It feels like constant tingling and often a bit of numbness – essentially frostbite. The feet are always uncomfortable. Raynaud's syndrome similarly affects the fingers.

When I saw the photos from that shoot, another strange change became obvious: my ears were much lighter in color than everything else – almost completely white. I realized I had seen it in the mirror but hadn't "registered" what I was looking at.

CHAPTER THREE

Diagnosis: Part 1

The test you never want to pass

Before my diagnosis, every blood test showed normal results. One doctor prescribed a liver function test to determine if there was excess protein in my urine, which she thought might explain the fluid retention. It wasn't the most pleasant experience, having to pee into a large brown jug with a handle (mercifully!) a certain number of times during a 24-hour period and store it in the fridge until I returned to the office. I got it wrong the first time. *Lucky me*, I got to do it *twice*! She also recommended cod liver oil to help with the swelling and my low vitamin D level.

I pressed on, working, studying, hanging out with friends as I could.

In 2006, I moved into another apartment. At this point, the skin color on my face had already started to change and I always felt weak and discouraged. One day, I looked in the mirror and noticed a few white spots on my face; they seemed to have appeared overnight. One at the inner corners of each eye and a fuzzy one at each outer corner of my mouth. What could I do? It was like an out-of-body experience. Innately, I knew that it must have something to do with how I was feeling and all the other things I was seeing. It couldn't be a coincidence that an increasing number of bizarre things was happening to me at the same time. I knew something was horribly wrong, but I didn't know what to do about it. Looking in the mirror, there was a dull feeling of hopelessness. I didn't know what to do. Over the next few months, the condition worsened, with my face looking burnt – black and "crispy" – with the white spots sharply contrasting against the dark everywhere else. My head looked smaller to me as, I supposed, the skin had become more tight and rigid. I developed stretch marks on my inner elbows because the skin was so tight it pulled when I straightened my arms. No amount of moisturizing relieved what I thought was extreme dryness. And it looked as though my actual bone structure had changed. Little did I know, I would see my appearance morph drastically many times over the next few years.

It's the Mystique in me

In the movie *X-Men*, Rebecca Romijn plays the shape-shifting mutant, Mystique. In her natural state Mystique looks like a blue snake/lizard creature with a human-like form. Her special ability is being able to mutate into a replica of any human, male or female. In the words of Rose Nylund, "Different on outside, same on inside." That's how I felt. I never knew what I would look like when I woke up. I could sometimes hardly recognize myself in the mirror but I was still me. I would stare at my reflection in wonder at how my face morphed from week to week, sometimes day to day. Disfigured by inflammation, skin tightening, pigment deformity, and broken capillaries. Ashen skin. Swollen eyelids. My stomach poked out like I was pregnant. I got dark spots all over my arms. I felt like a mutant except that I couldn't control how or when it would happen and it didn't give me any powers. But I was used to being noticed. I was used to being flirted with. That stopped happening. I felt invisible, masked by this exterior taking over me.

DIAGNOSIS: PART 1B

During the year when the darkening happened, I was studying acting. Constantly self-conscious, I told a friend in the class about my frustrations at not getting an answer about my appearance. I told her I had no idea what was happening or what to do. She asked, "Why don't you go to the Skin of Color Center?" "I never heard of it," I said. "Where is it?" "St. Luke's. But I think they're only open on Tuesdays," she said. It's a good thing I was working at CBS on the far West Side then because St. Luke's was not far up the street. In my research, I discovered that the center was co-founded by a dermatologist I used to visit in Philly for my PCOS-related issue, Dr. Susan Taylor, but she would not be my doctor there.

I met Dr. Andrew Alexis on a Tuesday in 2007, during my lunch break. From what I remember, I showed him the areas of most concern other than my face – the stretch marks in my elbows and especially the large area around my neckline from front to back covered with white little circles that blended together, each little circle centered with a speck of brown. It looked like a halo. He said, "You have scleroderma." His words were music to my ears! After more than a year of searching for something to hold on to, Dr. Alexis immediately recognized what was wrong! I didn't have to explain anything. He didn't deny my experience. I literally broke down in tears of relief – the tears I wouldn't let flow before – and said, "So you can fix it?!" I thought it would be like all of my other experiences with the doctor – get a diagnosis, then treatment, then cure and move on with my life. He briefly glanced downward and suggested that I allow his intern to do a biopsy – a small sample of skin from where the patch was on my upper back. I agreed.

St. Luke's is another teaching hospital. On the follow-up visit to get the result of the biopsy, I was in a situation that I would repeatedly find myself in, going forward. The room was filled with interns staring at me. Dr. Alexis said I had a condition known as "scleroderma." He said I would have to go to a rheumatologist. "Okay!" I was just so happy to have a name for what was happening and pleased that I could finally have a real plan to deal with this problem and "fix it." So, I was more than happy to agree to go to a 'rheumatologist,' whatever that was.

The primary blood test used to diagnose autoimmune diseases, as far as I know, is called the antinuclear antibody test (ANA). Antinuclear antibodies are produced by the immune system when it confuses the body's tissue for foreign bodies that need to be destroyed. That test, along with the visible symptoms, is how the specific autoimmune disorder is identified. In the words of Carrie Bradshaw, "I couldn't help but wonder," *why couldn't any one of those other doctors think of that?* I am probably being unfair to doctors, but I don't understand why they don't check the patient's ANA level in cases where they can't find an answer with run-of-the-mill bloodwork when certain symptoms are present: unexplained swelling, fatigue, and skin changes. Instead of doing one little test they deny or doubt what the patient is telling them and send them on their way when those tests come back normal. Yet, the experts say that early detection and treatment are key to a more favorable long-term prognosis. I don't understand the medical system at all.

One step forward, two steps back

My first rheumatologist was at St. Luke's. He explained to me exactly what scleroderma was. It was very hard to believe. He was telling me that I had an illness that would be progressive and potentially terminal and that it would never go away. *But, how?* What did *I* do? My initial happiness at having an answer quickly faded when I found out it only led to more confusion. The medications I would be taking would not reverse this illness. It was all about waiting and seeing how my body reacted. It was very discouraging. And those medications would have potentially serious side effects, a reality with which I would become intimately familiar in a few short years.

So, the search for an answer would *continue*, actually.

When you have a severe chronic illness, you become very aware of the wide and often hostile divide in healthcare between two approaches – allopathic and traditional/alternative medicine. The chronic illness world is no exception to conspiracy theories about collusion between doctors and the pharmaceutical industry to put profit before ending human suffering, and the attitude of some doctors doesn't help to quell that cynicism. Early in my illness, I had to scour the internet in a desperate search for positive, hopeful news about how I could deal with this. I searched for topics like "swelling," "unexplained swelling," "swollen legs," "shiny swollen skin," and everything else I could think of. That's how I found out about pitting edema. But none of the internet search results quite described what was happening to me in totality. In the meantime, I tried many "alternative" therapies to see what could work for me without toxic pharmaceuticals.

You don't know what you don't know, so you don't know exactly what or where to look.

Race for the cure: Pre-diagnosis edition

There's an aspect of my personality that proved to be vitally important in my journey with scleroderma, especially at the very beginning. I have always been a very inquisitive person, a bookworm and an information junkie. I enjoy learning new things for the sake of it and I am very good at finding information. I'm REALLY good at finding hard-to-find, obscure information that hardly anybody would know or care about. So, I was able to find a wide range of very useful information over the first few years. Knowledge comforts me.

Before diagnosis, I isolated each problem and went about getting treated for what I thought could be the source. This included many treatments that weren't strictly "medical," such as those listed below. But before I get started, I must point out an important caveat. There are many foods and supplements containing nutrients that combat inflammation, gut lethargy, weight and fatigue issues, sleeplessness, and other problems. However, my conclusion is that these are most effective in people who are already healthy. I believe they are best for the maintenance of good health and prevention of disease. But, when the immune system attacks the body it is meant to protect, the body enters a literal state of emergency, at which point holistic remedies alone are not likely to be effective, in my opinion. I believe it's important to attack the problem aggressively and as soon as possible with man-made Western pharmaceuticals while supporting the body with the healing and supportive nutrients provided by mother nature and continuing the search for a breakthrough.

Colonic

One of the very first ideas that occurred to me about my new swelling problem was that I must have a blockage somewhere in my system that was causing me to retain fluid, keep bloating, and feel lethargic. I assumed that my lymphatic system wasn't draining properly or my colon was backed up, or a combination of both. So I decided to try having my colon flushed. I made an appointment with a lady on Manhattan's Upper East Side. Honestly, I don't remember all the details, as it was a long time ago, but I must have had to remove my bottoms and lay on a table on my side, I think. The lady obviously had to insert a tube to flush water into my system that was immediately flushed out. I think it was a two-way tube. I do remember her telling me that I would be able to look at the clear tube and see undigested refuse flushing out. I didn't see anything. The procedure was, of course, entirely ineffective.

Naturopathy

My first inquiry into alternative medicine was at the office/store of what I am calling a naturopathic doctor at a shopping center on City Line Avenue in Philly. This was during the second year after the onset of my symptoms. My body and face were extremely swollen and I always felt hot, like I had a fever. I also felt the heaviness of the excess fluid particularly in my hands as they hung at my sides.

I explained to the practitioner what was wrong and he told me I had a chronic condition caused by inflammation. He explained to me that my blood cells were malformed. He showed me a drawing of what my red blood cells would look like. He took some blood and showed me my malformed red blood cells. But he couldn't specifically identify what was causing my problems. He just recommended anti-inflammatory supplements such as bromelain and other products to support my immune system. To be honest, I was never a good pill taker and I was skeptical about how supplements alone could stop what was happening to me. This seemed to be just a small piece of a large, complicated puzzle. The supplements did not result in any noticeable improvement.

Allergist

My search for healing before diagnosis also led me to an allergist near the Time Warner building on the Upper West Side. I wanted to find out if I had developed food allergies or an allergy to something else. He pricked the skin on my forearm with a small amount of about twenty allergens, including animal originated, in a pattern. I was to return in a day or two to see what reactions I had, if any. When I returned there were a couple of little bumps on my arm. Nothing alarming. I found out that I am allergic to lamb and cockroaches. I don't want to know what he put on my skin to figure out the latter! Another dead end.

Chinese medicine

The main reason I explored Chinese medicine is because of my impression that that tradition recognizes the body as one unit in which everything is interconnected. It's about bringing the body back into balance. I've had great doctors, and I don't mean to be so critical, but our medical system takes the opposite approach. I believe this is the reason most tend not to connect the dots and recognize that the myriad ailments described by a patient like me are likely inter-related. This blind spot typically results in a long lead time in disease progression before getting a diagnosis; a lot happens in the first two years, including anxiety, depression, and terror. In the meantime, you're left to fend for yourself. So I had no other choice but to look far and wide:

> Acupuncture
>
> Stress is one suspected catalyst for the series of biological events that leads to autoimmune disease. Acupuncture is known to help reduce stress, among providing many other benefits, so I thought I'd give it a try. I went to an acupuncturist in Midtown Manhattan, a Chinese gentleman who was very pleased to hear me talk about my appreciation for the holistic approach of Eastern medicine. The key with acupuncture is to get treated regularly; it's definitely a gradual process where the effect is supposed to be compounded over time. The truth is I only went once. Part of the reason is that my funds were very limited and it was not covered by insurance. But it also seemed like this approach was too mild for the severity of the problem I was facing.
>
> Herbs
>
> I went to a Chinese herbalist in Park Slope, Brooklyn, who recommended making a tea with an herb that came in little hard balls that were supposed to melt in hot water. They never melted no matter how hot the water, and I didn't know what I was drinking, anyway. It was hard to talk to the lady. I think she gave me a placebo.

CHAPTER FOUR

Diagnosis Part 2: The Road Back

There is a thing called "***anecdotal evidence***." It is described as follows on Wikipedia:

> *... Evidence collected in a casual or informal manner and relying heavily or entirely on personal testimony.*
> *... When compared to other types of evidence, anecdotal evidence is generally regarded as limited in value due to a number of potential weaknesses, but may be considered within the scope of the scientific method as some anecdotal evidence can be both empirical and verifiable, e.g. in the use of case studies in medicine. Other anecdotal evidence, however, does not qualify as scientific evidence, because its nature prevents it from being investigated by the scientific method. Where only one or a few anecdotes are presented, there is a larger chance that they may be unreliable due to cherry-picked or otherwise non-representative samples of typical cases. Similarly, psychologists have found that due to cognitive bias people are more likely to remember notable or unusual examples rather than typical examples. Thus, even when accurate, anecdotal evidence is not necessarily representative of a typical experience. Accurate determination of whether an anecdote is typical requires statistical evidence. Misuse of anecdotal evidence is an informal fallacy and is sometimes referred to as the "person who" fallacy ("I know a person who..."; "I know of a case where..." etc.) which places undue weight on experiences of close peers which may not be typical.*[5]

It's important that you grasp this concept before you read the rest of this section. As I mentioned previously, there is allopathic medicine and there is naturopathic medicine; the latter is often characterized as unreliable and even bogus due to its lack of formal scientific research such as peer-review, double-blind studies, and verifiable statistical data. Consistent, fairly predictable results across a large, diverse population are largely missing in the "natural medicine" world. But patients, of course, always have the freedom of choice in how to manage their health.

Dr. Andrew Weil is a well-known pioneer in 'integrative medicine' in the United States. A Philly native, he is often seen on PBS speaking on natural health. He has written many books, including *Natural Health, Natural Medicine*; *Eight Weeks to Optimum Health*; *Mind Over Meds;* and *Spontaneous Healing*. Integrative medicine is described on his website as "healing-oriented medicine" that involves a holistic approach to treat not just the body but also lifestyle elements that play a role in a person's health status.

In episode #350 of *The Tim Ferriss Show* podcast[6], Dr. Weil had this to say about double-blind, placebo-controlled studies:

> *It's one kind of information. And it has its own limitations. I think there are other kinds of information that are valid. For example, the information that comes from your own experience. And I like to point out to people that in all languages derived from Latin, unfortunately not English, the word for experience and the word for experiment are the same. In Spanish, 'experimentar' means both to experience and to experiment. So your own experience is a form of experimentation that produces useful information. You have to check it against other kinds of information. With double-blind studies, this is held out as the gold standard. And many people think this is the only kind of information we should pay attention to. But here's an interesting thing. You can try this yourself. And it's an assignment that I give to medical students and doctors.*
>
> *Go into a medical library and pull out any medical journal that reports results of placebo control double-blind testing. Pick an article. Turn to the back of the article where there's a table summarizing the results. In the placebo group, there will always be one or two or a small number of subjects who show all of the changes produced in the experimental group who got the drug.*
>
> *That is fascinating. That means that any change that we can produce in the human organism by giving a pharmacological agent can be exactly mimicked in at least some people some of the time purely by a mind-mediated mechanism, the placebo response if you want. Anyway, we*

should be trying to take advantage of that, find out how to make it happen more of the time. Also, I would just say that there are a great many worthless and dangerous drugs on the market at the moment. And many of them have a lot of placebo-controlled randomized trials behind them supporting their use. So things can be structured in ways to produce results that people want.

Then Tim posed the following question:

[You have found yourself] straddling what, at times people perceive to be mutually exclusive worlds: And I would love to hear – you've spoken I think quite a bit about some of the limitations of the types of studies we're talking about among others we haven't even talked about but that these are not necessarily the first place to go if you're looking to generate hypotheses that are innovative for testing in the first place. But if we were to flip the coin and look at the other side because you mentioned tone earlier and how a lot can be dismissed if you are angry and it's not a response to the content, but it's a response to the tone, where do people in the integrative medicine field or in the complementary or alternative treatment realms make mistakes? What are some of the ways in which they think they have all the answers or alienate themselves from people who might actually be open with a different delivery to some of what they're experimenting with?

Dr. Weil replied:

... I always emphasize just not being angry and to have some published data to support things that you're doing with patients so that if somebody asks why are you giving this treatment, you can cite something. So I think, to me, that's most important. I don't see many people today – the common mistake is just to antagonize colleagues or to reject conventional medicine out of hand. I don't like the term alternative medicine. It suggests that you're trying to replace conventional medicine. And that's not my goal. I want to make conventional medicine better. And knowing when and when not to use that system is extremely important. ... When you're dealing with people with chronic illness, whether it's chronic pain or autoimmunity where they don't see a possibility of changing it, you can, I think, arrange conditions of set and setting with the right agent in which you can show people that it's possible to experience your body in a different way.

"Anecdotal evidence" is a term often employed to express doubt toward patients' claims about the success of a treatment, with only a hint of condescension. However, when you are in the middle of a state of emergency, fighting for your very life, you don't really care about statistics and double-blind studies. You *need* to try as many options as possible, as responsibly as possible, to "fix it." You scour the internet in a desperate search for answers you can't get from your doctor. Because, after going through the heartbreak and anxiety of having the experts doubt your credibility, you develop a healthy mistrust of their judgment. Then every criticism about *their* credibility, rightly or wrongly, takes on a ring of truth: accusations like "they're pushers for the pharmaceutical industry, which needs people to remain sick for profit" are pretty common. This is what led me to...

THE ANTIBIOTIC PROTOCOL

I found out about this treatment from the good 'ole internet. I read about Dr. Thomas M. Brown, who pioneered and documented it in *The Road Back*. The book is about his use of low dose tetracyclines to reverse rheumatoid arthritis. As scleroderma is also a rheumatic illness, the treatment proved successful for those of his patients with this condition as well. I found out about Dr. Brown after my research initially led me to a book called *Scleroderma – The Proven Therapy That Can Save Your Life*, by Henry Scammell. This book is based on a single, small study that was published in a medical journal called *The Lancet*. Dr. Brown believed that connective tissue diseases, such as scleroderma, were caused by a small bacterium known as mycoplasma. His theory was that these bacteria settle in the connective tissue, multiply and die off, which releases toxins that trigger the dreaded inflammatory response that leads to autoimmunity. He was able to isolate this bacteria by withdrawing fluid from the joint of one of his arthritis patients and, thus, began his work healing scores of patients seemingly miraculously with an antibiotic called minocycline. The book documents these experiences. I cannot begin to tell you how excited I was to find out about this treatment.

Searching for a lifeline

Desperation will lead us to take chances that can be reckless. It can be argued that, whatever course of action we choose to take with an autoimmune disease, there will always be some level of risk. Pharmaceutical remedies have the potential for serious side effects and don't address the root cause of the illness. There is a standard approach to treatment – drugs to suppress the overactive immune system and counter-act the domino effect of thickening connective tissue on the skin and internal organs. Examples of the normal treatments are Cellcept, Methotrexate, Gabapentin, and Plaquenil (for lupus).

Getting a doctor to even consider a conversation about an alternative treatment turned out to be an effort in futility. Honestly, it was uncomfortable to even bring it up because of the expectation of doubt and cynicism. It's like saying you believe in unicorns or you can fly. You don't want to sound like you're going off the deep end. But I understand that there is a standard of care that's in the best interest of both parties. Also, being a litigious society, I expect that doctors probably also fear being sued if something goes wrong if they go off the beaten path.

I decided to try the Antibiotic Protocol. Antibiotics are widely prescribed, pretty safe and the protocol calls for a very low dosage. What was the worst that could happen? But I didn't want to go it alone; I'm not a medical professional. I didn't know about these things. I wanted my rheumatologist to check my blood and symptoms along the way and help me to document my progress, good or bad. I approached the topic very gingerly with the rheumatologist I had at that point, but he shook his head with a meager smile on his face. Later, my *favorite* rheumatologist literally said to me, "I don't think it will help you." I'm pretty sure she hadn't read anything about it and had probably never even heard of it. She didn't seem to know what I was talking about and, if she did, she gave no indication. That reaction was particularly disappointing, not to mention insulting, considering the lack of consideration. I knew I *had to* go it alone. At the back of my mind, I thought about the "I told you so" my doctors would give me if this didn't heal me or made matters worse...
... Which it did.

This is not a story of how the Antibiotic Protocol saved my life

Dr. Brown had long passed away. Dr. David Trentham, however, was still practicing in Boston and I wanted to book an appointment to see him. I called the office and they sent me paperwork to fill out before my visit.

My goal was to see Dr. Trentham ASAP, but I did not actually make an appointment because the logistics and economics were too stressful to handle on my own. It's funny how people around you can seem not as bothered by what you're going through as you might expect or hope; it's always good to have somebody in your corner who is engaged, proactive, and supportive. I decided to look for a doctor closer by, in the Philadelphia area, who was both a scleroderma specialist and used the protocol. I came across a sort of chat room online about scleroderma. There was a thread about the Antibiotic Protocol and someone asked where they could find a doctor who would be willing to treat them. Someone mentioned a doctor just outside of Philadelphia – across the street from West Philadelphia, in fact – who had actually been a resident of Dr. Brown's. I was elated! This doctor was just fifteen minutes away from my house! I thought my prayers were answered. I immediately found his information and called his office. When I found out where he was located, I realized it was a building I had driven by probably hundreds of times.

The feeling of familiarity can be misleading. It can create a feeling of trust and safety prematurely. When we feel safe, we let our guard down. That, with the desperation for a solution to a life-threatening problem, is what can make seeking out alternative options to the status quo very risky. The extent of my research into this doctor was, to be quite honest, his website; the (presumably truthful) testimonials on the internet; and my office consultation with him. The initial consultation had to take place in a far off rural suburb over an hour away, for some reason. At the appointment, where I expected a medical office with a nurse who would take my blood, etc., I found a converted house packed with people in the waiting area. I saw faces filled with expectation and restrained anxiety. My appointment with the doctor didn't quite go as expected. He "prescribed" a very large amount of dietary supplements by a company called Cal-Amo. I don't believe he actually explained how they would help me. But I do remember the sticker shock: $300 on my credit card. The next step was to see him on the Main Line for the treatment.

I was very excited and full of hope about my upcoming appointment with the doctor, who was basically in my neighborhood. I took the day off from work to see him. The office was on the main thoroughfare that separates Philadelphia from Montgomery County. I turned into the parking lot from the busy street and entered the brown building. What immediately came to mind when I saw the interior was an economical hotel lobby. As I recall, from the doorway to the left there was a wall of windows as well as cushioned built-in seating running its length, on which several people were seated. There was a long desk to the right of that and another tall one directly in front of the front door. To the left of the desk in front, there seemed to be a darkened hallway. To the right, between the two desk areas, was a hallway where the patient rooms were, the first of which was visible from the entrance. That was the one where I met with the doctor.

The appointment was peculiar. The conversation meandered a bit from the bacterial infection causing inflammatory diseases like scleroderma to how his license was always under threat because of his outsider status in the medical community. He shrugged it off with a defiant, "They can take my license!" but it was a bit unnerving. My concerns grew with the lack of basic medical procedures I was used to. He didn't seem to have a nurse, he didn't check my blood pressure, weight or pulse, but he whipped out an old-school mercury-filled thermometer to take my temperature; I hoped he had washed it before putting it in my mouth.

The other thing that really bothered me was the interference in our conversations by his "assistant," a devotee who claimed to have been cured of lupus through his treatment. It was bizarre because he never controlled the conversation whenever she was around. I would ask him a question and she would loudly interject, even repeatedly cutting him off, and he would just stand there. During my first treatment, I was calmly watching some talk show on the TV bolted to the wall close to the ceiling when she insisted I watch something else and changed the channel. It was all very disconcerting, but I figured if the treatment worked to cure my disease it wouldn't really matter. I think that's what most people must think.

The Antibiotic Protocol is not covered by insurance if it's not administered by an allopathic medical doctor, so I had to pay out of pocket. I don't remember how much it cost but it was at least a couple hundred per treatment.

I arrived for my first treatment in the fall of 2009. I was supposed to eat before going but I forgot, so I grabbed breakfast from McDonald's across the street. The assistant lady scolded me for drinking orange juice, which is bad for the condition. The medication is administered through an IV drip over the course of an hour. I sat in the cushioned recliner and either she or the doctor hooked the IV up to my left arm. That's where my "good vein" was. I didn't feel any different when it was over. There was to be a course of several treatments given over either weekly or bi-weekly intervals (I don't remember) until the progress became apparent, at which point I believe the dosage would be tapered off.

But, soon after that first treatment, trouble began. Before beginning the treatment, my disease had been scary but pretty stable. I had many of the normal symptoms, like painful finger ulcers, mental fog, severe fatigue, muscle wasting and, of course, skin changes. Even with that, I was still managing it with my doctor. I started coughing, had fevers, and developed a rash all over my face. My face looked red and I was always sweaty. At first, I thought it was a manifestation of scleroderma but realized it must be something else. I called the office in a panic one day on my way home on Amtrak, describing what was happening to me. I believe I went to the office directly from the train station. We didn't go into a room for him to evaluate me – we just talked in the front area. Anyway, he certainly didn't seem very concerned. He told me to take Benadryl. He did not say the word "allergy." He just told me to take Benadryl to deal with my symptoms. Because of the lack of – how do you call it? Medical rigor? Procedural integrity? – the basic normal medical protocol I had come to expect, combined with the behavior of this doctor and his staff, I decided to stop seeing him and ran to my already-skeptical rheumatologist, expecting to hear the version of "I told you so" she would have for me.

It triggered lupus.[7]

That was how I found out I am allergic to minocycline. My condition deteriorated significantly and, in 2009, I was diagnosed with lupus overlap which changed my diagnosis to mixed connective tissue disease.

CHAPTER FIVE

Every Little Step I Take

In the middle of all of this, I was commuting to work from Philly to New York. I would wake up at five a.m. and drag myself out of bed. The best I could do most mornings was brush my teeth and get dressed. The rest of my energy was for making it to the bus at the corner of 60th and Master, which, mercifully, was only a few footsteps away. But it was still a daily struggle to make it to the 6:15 bus on time. The journey was one obstacle and test of endurance after another. And it was a harsh education in the many microaggressions the disabled must deal with when encountering the public. At times it can be genuinely dangerous.

The first hurdle was always getting the SEPTA bus driver – the same guy every day – to let the air out of the front tire to lower the bus so that I could board. My rigid leg muscles could not step up high enough without the assistance, at least not without a lot of difficulty. He made me ask every. Single. Morning. One morning, when I once again asked him to lower the bus he huffed at me in an aggressive tone, "Ma'am, it's not working today!" I grabbed the metal bars on both sides of the steps and pulled myself up onto the first step. He pulled off before I could sit and, of course, I couldn't keep my balance at that point so I sat down before I could pay. In New York, the drivers lower the buses immediately without anyone having to prove the necessity, so it was always frustrating that, in Philadelphia, they treated this minor, basic service as some sort of privilege a passenger has to earn according to the driver's personal assessment. They don't even lower the bus for mothers and their children, but that's a different story.

There is one experience I will never forget. But it culminated two of my deepest vulnerabilities – being both disabled and a Black woman. I was able to drag my miserable self from Penn Station to the Q train at Herald Square to get to my meeting planning job at Union Square. The stairway down to the station from the park across from the mall is very narrow and, during rush hour, it's very close quarters. I was walking down the stairs like everybody else. But it was New York, survival of the fittest. I was holding on to the metal banister to keep steady when, out of nowhere, a White guy decided to take advantage of the sliver of space between the two lines of people – one going up and the one I was in, going down – to force his way ahead of everybody else to get to the street. But I was the only one he knocked himself into. I paused briefly. But, as I was recovering, a Latino guy holding a heavy backpack, whom I presumed to be Mexican, followed suit. However, he did one better and rammed his entire left side into me almost knocking me down the steps. A woman in the other line looked at me in shock, shaking her head. She said something to me but we both continued on our way. It didn't hurt much, but it did knock the wind out of me. In a stairway packed with people, I was *the only one* they did this to.

And walking was becoming more and more... difficult, since the antibiotic fiasco. If I could think of a far stronger word, I would use it. Difficult is an understatement. Along with the physical issues that made walking feel like fighting against a strong current with the needle on my energy tank sinking past E, there was also a distinct sensation haunting me. A different kind of weight. This one was not in my body. It felt like it was something in the ether, a dark cloud, a spirit, something sinister pulling at me, hovering over me, and I could not escape. I couldn't out-walk it, I couldn't out-run it. It was not tangible. I couldn't see it. This dark thing had me in its grasp, enveloping me, trying to take me down. I had to fight that, too.

I would get to my job and be almost completely useless. All of my energy, concentration, and will were spent by the time I got there and plopped down into my chair in relief. My mental fog was getting worse. At the time I didn't know that was what it was. I just knew my thinking was very slow. And it was happening at the very worst time possible, right when I was in the middle of helping to plan the organization's annual conference. This planning involved several teams that had to communicate regularly via conference calls and in-person meetings, and part of my responsibility was to coordinate all communications, summarize them, and regularly update the group. That was in addition to my regular work on a national initiative. I wasn't the best at my job at that time.

I didn't know anything about disability benefits. I began to call myself "disabled" but I didn't know anything about filing for disability benefits or if I would even qualify. My idea of a disabled person was the same as everybody else's: an elderly person with trouble moving around or someone who had lost a limb, diminished use of a part of their body, blindness – something everyone can see. The idea of "invisible disability" never occurred to me. I just knew that I was having extreme difficulty with the functioning of my body and a deterioration in my quality of life. Since I could still get up and go to work most days, though, I figured that's what I had to do until I couldn't anymore. Now, I know that is not true, and I could have qualified at that time and received benefits while still working as much as I could.

I was the weird girl at work. That's how I felt. Nobody said anything or treated me poorly but I did feel... other. I was moved to the rear area of the office, in front of the Vice President's corner office and two feet in front of the small break room. The ceiling in that section of the office was much lower. The area had an abundance of fluorescent light, unlike the front where there were large windows letting in natural light. Directly above me were four sets of fluorescent lights – the long ones – in addition to the two in the break room and the others I faced to the right throughout the open space office. This is how I found out I had developed an "allergy" to fluorescent light. I started to get daily headaches. One bright and sunny day, I wore my bright and sunny yellow sweater T-shirt to Chelsea Piers to scout a potential location for an event. As I sat in the waiting area for the lady to give me a tour, I started seeing the telltale squiggly lines in the bottom half of my vision. I started to panic. I knew what was coming. Soon I started to get that itchy sort of feeling and pressure in my head. By the time the woman FINALLY came to greet me, I was officially in migraine mode. I willed myself to pay attention and get through the visit as fast as possible. I had to walk back to the bus stop, get on the bus, then walk down from the bus stop to the building, take the elevator to my floor, walk to the office, and settle into my chair. Every moment was agony and panic. By that point, I could barely see anything and the unbearable pain had set in. I told the VP I had a migraine. Thankfully the President wasn't there that day and I could sit in his dark office. I think I took Excedrin for migraine. But sit I didn't. I crawled on my hands and knees, I rested my head on the glass coffee table at times because it was cool, I sweated, I buried my face in the couch, I prayed for forgiveness for every sin I committed. And I groaned. I groaned loudly. In the President's office. At work. At least I didn't vomit. There is NO pride in illness. The next day, the VP said I had given him a scare. Of course, the whole ordeal had completely left my mind by then, but I apologized. My life... I don't know if my health challenges made me more susceptible to these headaches.

Once or twice, I had to call out from work because I literally couldn't walk at all. The tendons in my inner arches would suddenly seize up, like how you might pull a drawstring to close a bag as tight as possible. My feet would become immobile and it was painful. I assume this was related to neuropathy.

CHAPTER SIX

Living With Scleroderma

Show and tell, for chrissake!

I was what you might call a "bad" patient. I was one of those patients who put on a brave face for her doctor. I did not talk to my fave rheumy, Dr. Natalie Azar, about the severe trouble I had with energy and the functioning of my legs. I did not tell her about being so overcome with exhaustion at work that I dragged myself to the park just across the street from her office to take a nap on a bench. My one-hour lunch break often became a two-hour break because it was so difficult to pull the energy together to raise my body to sit up then stand. I did not tell her about feeling like I was walking against a strong tide, to the extent that I dreaded crossing the street to get to that park and back again. I prayed I would not pass out and get run over by a taxi while crossing 6th Avenue.

Dr. Azar referred me to a cardiologist at Cornell Medical Center. My mother came with me as it would have been impossible to get there by myself. My mother was my chaperone, CNA, and patron. On this occasion, we took the train as the repeated cab rides added up quite a bit. The 72nd Street stop on the 6 train does not have an elevator. I dreaded walking up that long flight of steep steps in the midst of aggressive able-bodied New Yorkers. My mom was close behind me. I just hoped that most people would walk around us, hoped it would be obvious that I was having trouble. For the most part, that's what happened. Until one vocal individual, a senior citizen, a White lady, angrily growled something at me about getting out of the way. When I could get some extra breath in my lungs after the shock, I yelled at her that I was disabled, not that she cared. But when I got to the cardiologist, after a lot of miscommunication by her office's staff causing us to walk in circles, I told her about how hard it was to walk. She asked if I had told Dr. Azar and I said I hadn't, feeling kind of embarrassed and silly. She suggested that: 1) I tell Dr. Azar and 2) it may be a problem with a protein (the name of which I don't remember) in my muscles. I believe I had a form of inflammatory myopathy but was never diagnosed since I never told my doctors about it.

The location of the hospital made it hard to get a cab going back west. They're not allowed to stop on that avenue going uptown and, as I recall, the bus on that street comes eastward. So, you have to walk. I've never been a fan of the East Side because of the crappy transit options. Maybe there was another way to get back to the train but, if there was, it wasn't apparent. I just wanted to get home as soon as possible. If you know what it's like for your legs to go numb and still have to walk, it was something like that. And it was scary. I had to stop frequently. Once I sat on a bench in front of a restaurant. When we made it down the first flight of stairs into the train station, I was pretty sure I would pass out. Thankfully I didn't because I was able to rest against a stone barrier at the landing.

Invisible me

In the early days of scleroderma, I wanted to wear a sign that read, "This is not the real me!" Or a mask of my pre-scleroderma appearance. I wanted to be seen as what I thought to be my true self, not this involuntary sickly version that didn't belong to me as far as I was concerned. I felt hidden. I was no longer noticed. I was no longer seen as beautiful, apparently. The feeling of being invisible was very new and depressing. Fast forward a few years and now people say things like, "You have BEAUTIFUL skin!" and "Your skin is so smooth." One lady repeatedly complimented me for my smooth, clear skin. Sometimes women ask me what products I use. Compliments are supposed to make you feel good, but I have been reluctant to take them as intended because that seems fraudulent, too. I've had to learn to appreciate this new image. I've come a long way! I keep remembering what an old boyfriend would often tell me: "You're *so hard on yourself*!"

In the movie, *The House Bunny*, Anna Faris plays a dim-witted Playboy Bunny who found a job as a sorority's house "mother" after being kicked out of the Playboy mansion. In the final climactic scene, she gives testimony about how deceiving appearance can be:

> *I'm allergic to erythromycin.*
>
> *I took it once when I had a cold.*
> *I was 16, and it gave me itching.*
>
> *I mean, everything itched.*
> *My legs, my arms, my earlobes.*
>
> *And other stuff, too, but I can't say,*
> *because I'm live on the air right now,*
>
> *and you can't say "ass cheeks," right?*
>
> *... But besides the itching,*
> *the erythromycin also made my skin glow.*
>
> *It gave me, like, this glowing tan.*
>
> *And I suddenly felt like another person.*
>
> *Different.*
>
> *Better.*
>
> *Prettier, I guess.*
>
> *... Michelle, do you know that feeling*
> *that I'm talking about?*
>
> *Where you suddenly feel pretty*

and, next thing you know,
you feel better about yourself?

Well, that was what was happening to me.

My allergic reaction made me feel pretty,

and so I ignored all the bad side effects,
because suddenly people were talking to me

and they were noticing me.

And even though I was itching like crazy,

it was worth it to feel accepted.

And so I couldn't wait to get a cold
so I could take my erythromycin.

But underneath that beautiful, glowing skin,
I still had that cold.

Well, that's a meteor.

... It flashes by and burns bright,
but then it disappears.

And that was what was happening to me.

The real me just disappeared.[8]

Like minocycline, erythromycin is a tetracycline.

"Good days"

There were occasional shining threads of hope. Days when it was almost like nothing was wrong. We call these "good days." I don't know other people called them when they think about them in their heads. But that really was what other *scleros* called it.

On a good day, you can completely forget you have limitations. For a moment, your body gives you a break and you are free. One good day, I put on my leggings and sports bra and went outside to the front of the house with my jump rope. It was nighttime, dark outside, perhaps eight p.m. in the summer. I jumped rope for, maybe, ten minutes off and on. Then I grabbed the rake and raked the forest of leaves on our small lawn, creating two large piles. There was no pain, no fatigue, no panting.

The thing about good days is they come at a high cost. There is an almost immediate backlash by your body. I have spent two months or more recovering from a single good day. It's like your body implodes and every symptom comes back with a vicious vengeance. Every time that happened, I ended up in the ER. The most common reaction from aerobic activity was, and still is, a sharp, deep pain in the middle of my chest and difficulty breathing; it's similar to bronchitis or asthma.

I got better at spotting good days and monitoring my activity.

I was very concerned about the toll sitting and lying down all the time was taking on my body. I had already experienced wasting, which I noticed while I was still working and my body started getting smaller. I wanted to have an activity that was low impact, easy. I decided to try water aerobics. After all, it was an all-body workout that people say is easy on the joints. Everyone told me what a great idea it was. The YMCA was two blocks up the street. I joined. There was a class open to beginners two or three days a week. It wasn't long before I had to stop going. My symptoms got worse. I had to go back to the doctor.

Mind over matter?

Between the winter of 2010 and spring of 2012, I was in and out of the hospital, staying one and two weeks at a time with short visits to the ER in between. My only outings were church, doctor, and trips to the mall or to eat out with my mom. From Christmas break 2010 (more to come) to the spring of 2011, I spent the majority of my time in bed, immobile. My mother would bring breakfast to me on a tray before going to work in the morning. I would wait there all day for her to come back home so I could eat again. I would only get up to go to the bathroom, carefully unlocking limb after limb, forcing some flexibility into my muscles. Once there, I would have to wait so long to get the courage and energy together to try to get up that my legs would go numb. Sometimes my mom wouldn't get home until ten or eleven at night. That's when I would get to eat again unless there was something left on my tray.

You must be wondering what in the world I did all day lying in bed in a house by myself for twelve hours or more. You must be thinking, "how boring, lonely, and depressing." But it wasn't. And no, I didn't sleep the days away. You may be surprised to know, being that sick gives one a lot to think about. The things your body is going through and the effort to keep one's self going is all-consuming. You think about it all day long while you're awake. The only way to notice time going by is when the sunlight changes significantly as the day goes on. I liked the quiet. And I didn't want to figure out how to get out of bed for anything more than was minimally necessary.

My lung issues were not a mind-over-matter kind of thing, either.

Looking back, this quiet time prepared me for the ordeal soon to come. The most important thing you can have in a situation like that is a strong mindset. Your mindset is about both how you think and what you do. I realize now that my mindset was grounded in a set of routines. Routines give a sense of stability and a foundation for attempting to handle situations that come with uncertainty. Routine One was to get up, get well dressed, and go to church on Sunday. After service, my mom and I usually went out to lunch. Routine Two was the morning routine. My mom would wake me up to a tray of breakfast, usually tea, eggs, and toast with butter and jelly, or oatmeal. I would eat and watch the morning news or 80s crime shows on Hallmark either in bed or downstairs. My very favorite part of the morning was watching the game shows, especially *Let's Make A Deal.* You can't watch that show and not be energized and uplifted. If I didn't have appointments, the rest of the day was open.

Next to routines are other activities based around interests. It's important to have some way to take the focus off of one's self and cultivate a positive mindset. You have to make yourself happy. One of the activities that proved to be a great outlet for my creativity, passion, and skills was ministry. I was very active in the church, especially after I started getting better, and was very happy to give something back to the community that had been so important to me; I also felt it was my calling to use my talents and the free time I had to contribute to the Kingdom of God.

CHAPTER SEVEN

Do NOT Go To Bootcamp Disabled!

Maybe the real key to my recovery is stubbornness. True faith requires a kind of stubbornness: sticking to core principles and values in spite of the constant barrage of seductive temptations; believing in something without discernible, concrete evidence. If faith is a kind of stubbornness, or at least requires stubbornness, it would be the *good kind* of stubbornness. There is also the *bad kind* of stubbornness – the stubbornness that negates wisdom, compassion, empathy or grace; the stubbornness that leads to making decisions that may be reckless and counter-productive, even dangerous. I have had both kinds. Now, hopefully, far less of the latter.

For the first few years of this experience, my mind and my body were not in sync. My body was clearly in a state of desperate confusion. My mind was a bit behind – on the one hand, aware that something was very wrong, on the other not fully accepting it. As I told you, I had always been strong and capable of doing whatever I wanted to do. I had overcome many obstacles in my life. A boyfriend once called me "so resilient" because I always found a way to overcome a setback. That was my mindset, my understanding, my perspective. Me. I did not see this problem as being very different from any other, other than that it was more significant and I couldn't combat it on my own as usual. I became very frustrated with the state of my life and going through such tremendous challenges gave me a kind of boldness I hadn't really had before. I suppose I was compensating for the feeling that everything was falling apart and I wanted to take control. The other strong tide I was fighting was the feeling that the more I did, the less headway I was making. My efforts were futile against this enemy within.

I started to think about what I really wanted to do with my life. I had always been interested in shipping. I had wanted to train to be a seaman on cargo ships in my early twenties but I didn't think it was realistic for me. I had even done a little research to find out where I could learn about seafaring and found one school in Manhattan. I dropped the notion pretty fast because I just didn't believe I could do it. But, at that moment, thinking about what I really wanted brought it back. In 2010, I started to talk about this interest out loud for the first time in my life. Eventually, I mentioned it to the right person. I don't remember how the conversation went but, in casually talking about it to a board member of the non-profit where I worked, he mentioned that he was also a board member for the local maritime college, which I hadn't known existed. He made a phone call, gave me a recommendation, and I met with the Dean of the graduate program (I have a B.S. in Economics). All I had to do was fill out the application.

Here's the problem

Well, there were two problems, really:

1. I decided to do both the graduate program *and* the Regiment of Cadets
2. Being accepted into the reg. required medical clearance

The Regiment of Cadets is regarded as a "disciplined lifestyle program." Similar to the military, its purpose is to prepare students/cadets for the rigors and requirements of work onboard commercial vessels. Upon completion of the reg., which includes two summer sea terms on a training vessel, the cadet sits for the exams (written and physical) to earn a 3rd Mate deck or engine license with the U.S. Coast Guard. As you may imagine at this point, it is physically intensive, intended for the fittest and most youthful prospects. I was neither. But I was determined. I decided that my intention was to earn a deck license to gain insight into the work and life of a mariner and I would use that experience to inform my shore-side entrepreneurial pursuits.

About that medical clearance

The two doctors I approached for medical permission were my rheumatologist and my pulmonologist. When I showed them what I wanted to do, alarms naturally went off in their heads. My rheumy had once said, "I don't think you're taking this seriously," and those words must have come back to her then. She expressed her concerns. My pulmonologist literally said to me (not verbatim), "I don't want to sign this and have you drop dead when you get there." He definitely said the words, "drop dead," though. I cried in front of him and his resident, pleading, "I promise I won't die! (Hey, I kept my word didn't I?) It's the only thing I want to do." To cover himself, I'm sure, as well as to genuinely assess my fitness he had me re-do several tests, including a breathing test and a step test that involved climbing up and down four steps while the resident monitored my heart rate and blood flow with the pulse-ox on my finger. Both doctors signed off on the medical clearance and I was off to bite off more than I could reasonably chew. My brother, who was in the Navy, asked about me going to INDOC, "How are you going to do all that *like that*?" I shrugged and said, "I'll just do it." Oh boy!

Indoctrination – If it had not been for the Prednisone on my side...

It was the summer of 2010. The Regiment of Cadets begins with a 10-day indoctrination that is NOT for the faint of heart. It is similar to military boot camp and many cadets are interested in continuing on to the actual military; some were already in the ROTC. INDOC is unforgiving; cadets are startled awake from sleep for physical training (PT) at five a.m., showers are limited to two minutes, and there is non-stop activity all day long. There's training in firefighting, swimming, and watchkeeping, and deck work chipping paint. When I took my work gloves off in my room after the one time I spent the morning doing deck work, my hands looked, once again, like catcher's mitts. I didn't even feel it but I was petrified that somebody would see it. With inflammation raging, I had to bend my swollen knees and force my stiffened muscles to sit upright, "Indian style," for indeterminate amounts of time on a concrete floor with *teenagers* right out of high school. I was not only one of the relatively few females but I was likely also the oldest. Weird girl. A weird girl who literally could not run and had to sit out PT in the "broken" section. I kid you not.

You may be asking yourself, "how in the world did she make it through that ten days?" After once again struggling to make it off the concrete floor because my muscles couldn't bend (I will spare you the details of how I managed to do that), I realized that I had a solution: Prednisone! Prednisone was my best friend and having to take it gave me a break from the concrete test of endurance intended for people half my age.

On graduation day, I prayed that I would be able to hold it together. I was so tired. We had to march to the field and stand at attention ("Do *not* lock your knees!") for an hour or two on the field for the commencement. What a relief to get to the car and drive myself, my mom, my uncle, and my nephew home.

But wait! There's more.

Because of my stubbornness, I had to learn the hardest way possible to listen to my body. I have learned the importance of letting go of ego. So many embarrassing things happened that I could never write about. I had to develop a tunnel vision to get through and not be completely discouraged, to not give in to feelings of humiliation.

I only made it through one semester directly after INDOC – fall. It was winter time, and several times a week we had to wake up early, make our beds, and sometimes wait for inspection before going outside to the quad for formation before classes began. I walked to class in the rain, in strong winds, in shoes and a heavy wool pea coat that felt like they weighed a ton. Cadets had to walk a very specific path and, most of the time, we had to run from one corner to the other and cut each corner. Additionally, on the weekend and holidays, I would drive home two hours from New York to Philadelphia and back. It was the sustained physical strain that led to my first brutal reality check.

There's only so much Prednisone can do. It helped to almost eliminate the inflammation and gave me energy. It took the edge off. But I was pushing it too far. During that first semester, I began to experience mind-numbing throbbing pain all over my body. I would wake up stiff as a board every morning, practically unable to move from rigidity. My joints and my bones felt like they were welded together or made of glass and one false move would make me shatter, like Sam Jackson in *Unbreakable*. Every movement was excruciating, and I felt like a block of lead. I lost more weight. I feared going to sleep because of what I would face once I woke up. But the fatigue caused me to sleep like a coma.

I developed a persistent dry, heavy cough at some point.

Fatigue, atrophy, pain, sluggishness, and a hard cough. Things were pretty bad. But that was not the worst of it.

I developed a swelling on my right eye. I started wearing shades as it got worse over the course of the week. It got to be so heavy that I could barely hold my eye open. I went to the health office on campus but they suggested I go to the doctor down the street for an assessment. They were there for healthy-people problems. I went back to my dorm to drop off my bookbag but also left my phone. I didn't think I would need it. I figured, if anything, the doctor would give me a prescription and I would be right back. In my uniform, I drove to the little town. I parked my silver Toyota Matrix on a residential street with the windows cracked because it was still warm, one block over from the doctor's office. When I saw the doctor he joked, "Who punched you in the eye?" I told him nobody punched me. Nothing hit my eye. It just started swelling up. He told me I had an infection and I needed to go to the ER immediately. "I could have sworn something knocked you in the face." I left my car where it was and took the bus. I was admitted right away and spent a week there, being given antibiotics and fluid. But, remember, I had left my phone in the dorm. I hadn't told my roommate where I was going and, after a day, she got concerned so she found my mom's number in my phone and called her. My biggest concern, though, was missing my classes. The school was very strict. I had assignments due. We were not allowed to miss more than three days in a row without an excuse. I insisted that I couldn't stay. But there was no other choice. I found out that I could be excused for a medical emergency. I don't quite remember how I was able to tell my roommate where I was. I must have used the hospital phone to call the school or something. My mom had to come to New York with my uncle to get my car, with its windows that had been open for days, from in front of somebody's house. When I was discharged, I returned to school to finish the semester.

The road back, indeed

There comes a time when there is no other choice but to give up.

My final drive home from maritime school was Christmas break, 2010. I packed as much as I could into my car and headed back to the outskirts of Philly. I was low on gas but figured I'd stop on Admiral Wilson Boulevard, right before the Ben Franklin Bridge, because attendants in New Jersey pump the gas for you. That would spare me having to make extra movements getting in and out of my car. But I forgot and I didn't check my fuel level again until I was ten minutes away from home and, by then, the needle was almost under the last low mark. Concerned that my car would stall before I got home, I decided to stop and get a little bit of gas.

I knew I was stiff, but I did not expect the issue I encountered. I could not stand up. My body had practically solidified into the shape of the car seat that I had sat in for nearly two hours. I had to get out of the car hunched over, unable to fully straighten my legs or bend back at the waist to stand upright. Worse, the pump wouldn't accept cards so I had to walk into the store. What an odd sight I must have been! But the weirdest part (yes, there was something even weirder than that) was that as soon as I got out of the car, I saw a haggard looking woman walking *exactly* the same way! I thought, is this some kind of cosmic joke? Are you kidding me? I won't get into the stares I got from the guys working there.

By the time I was done pumping the gas, my limbs had softened a bit. At least, I wasn't riddled with anxiety for the last ten minutes of the drive. I parked my car directly across the street from our front door. My mom knew I was on my way and she must have been looking out the window because, when I looked across, she was standing at the open door. But I couldn't move. I sat for a couple of minutes trying to work out how I could possibly bring my things inside. I finally decided to leave it all. I slid off the seat and shut the door behind me, this time able to stand slightly but still hunched over. I said hi to my mom and went straight to bed. I would stay there for several months.

This was not a mind-over-matter situation.

I counsel you to buy from me gold refined by fire, so that you may be rich, and white garments so that you may clothe yourself and the shame of your nakedness may not be seen, and salve to anoint your eyes, so that you may see.
- Revelation 3:18

PART TWO

Purgatory

CHAPTER EIGHT

Diagnosis, Part 3

Never underestimate the power of the mind and the spirit.

This is a story about sight. About coming to a point where you realize you've been blind the whole time, walking around in blindness, darkness. It's about enlightenment. Having a light switched on to illuminate one's true reality. The truth about who you are, the truth about your purpose and the truth about what's possible. Living. The true meaning of living. My life was saved, first, when I became saved and, second, when I realized that I had to un-learn many lessons taught to me directly and subconsciously that kept me hiding my light under a bushel, as I was once told. Enlightenment has given me confidence, peace, and courage. Courage to embrace who I am. Courage to be vulnerable. Courage to forgive myself for the past. Courage to forgive others. And courage to believe in myself. That is not to say the work is complete. But part of the gift of a second chance was the opportunity to even get started on this work of self-renewal and transformation, and to continue. In many ways my life is a lot better now, after the storm, than it was before: I no longer wander without clarity, depressed and anxiety-ridden.

But, greater than what I have already told you, the greatest I have yet to mention – that the most precious thing I have gained is love for myself. This is how death saved my life.

In the spring of 2012, I was an oncology patient at the Hospital of the University of Pennsylvania, hanging on by sheer will and an army of prayer warriors – my New Life church family, my relatives, and my friends. Minister Mundgen sewed a prayer shawl. Elders visited me, prayed with me, and read the bible for me when I couldn't talk or stay awake. I pointed to the psalm I wanted to hear so Hermine could read it to me. Pastor Clark came regularly to pray with me and talk, just as she had when I had been house-bound. She told the congregation during a prayer that I sometimes didn't even know she was there. I was a testimony at New Life. A miracle. The congregation had witnessed the progression of my illness, first as a scleroderma sufferer, then as a scleroderma/cancer patient whose hat fell off during service to reveal my bald head. Some members were also members of the church I attended with Mrs. Lee. But it's what it had taken to make it to this point that I want to tell you about.

When words are inadequate

It's difficult to go back to that place in my mind. The night that I broke. The next day that I strained to grab hold of.

The weight of death was crushing. I observed it, at first, like a curiosity. Like when you watch a speeding car careen toward you and you freeze at first, as if to make sure you can believe what you're seeing, and then decide what to do. A brief pause of confusion and horror. So much was happening: I had terrible difficulty breathing; there was a pervasive, overwhelming, extreme tiredness that felt like it was even taking energy from my future. But, more than anything else, there was this other sensation... I struggled to describe it to myself. The closest I could come is the feeling of some *thing* trying to rip my entire being, my soul, right out of my body. Some *thing* trying to separate me from myself, pull me apart in every direction. Struggling for every breath gave the thing a discernible physical dimension. It made that deep, unidentifiable, terrifying sensation even more real. It was surreal. I had no frame of reference for this level of anguish, no language to express it, even to myself. The thought occurred to me, "words are inadequate." There are no words.

Desperation brought me to my proverbial knees. I had a strong sense of the reality that it was impossible for even the brightest minds and most advanced technologies alone to save me. The feeling of utter helplessness engulfed me. This should have caused me to sink into a deep depression and complete hopelessness. But my focus was always on the blood of Jesus and the promises of my Father in heaven. Those psalms, prayers, songs, and scriptures were my reassurance. My faith transcended the dark place into which I had descended. I could see a small, steady light at the end of the long and vast tunnel of darkness that enveloped me. I was exhausted from pushing against that powerful force and sensed myself losing my footing, slipping further and further away from freedom. I thought about how completely alone I was; that this was a singular experience and all the support and love and well wishes in the world could not replace it. No one could carry this burden with me. No one else could experience it. And I would never be able to fully explain it. I was alone. And it will always be a very painful memory. But...

There was a light. And no matter how small and far off it was, it was there.

This was the night I knew I had a choice to make. To live or to die. I had to make a decision. I will always remember this turning point. I thought, "I understand why people give up," but I prayed one simple prayer over and over again. I prayed for the next moment. I wasn't asking for the whole night or the next morning or even a future. I only prayed for the very next moment. Over and over again as I sat wrapped in layers of hospital blankets, with two pairs of non-slip hospital socks over my always-freezing feet. That was my meditation as I struggled to pull air into my nose and lungs. I had a feeding tube in by then. I received pure oxygen from a tube attached to my nostrils. And I focused on the light as I repeated this prayer for my very life until I eventually fell asleep.

Faith = Freedom

Getting closer to God gave me freedom in my confinement. Freedom allowed me to rest. I realized that if I wanted to win my survival, I had to give up. I had to let go. Giving up, I gained something that I know sounds impossible under these circumstances: joy. Joy in the middle of abject misery. I wasn't "happy." Joy is something very different from happiness. That was my second realization, that I didn't have to be happy to be full of joy. Happiness is circumstantial and regenerated through external factors; joy is grounded in spirit and mindset, which can dictate what the circumstance means to you and how you are affected by it. It is a position of empowerment in the most vulnerable of situations. I hadn't understood that when a friend had tried to explain it to me seven years before. Joy gave me confidence. Confidence gave me the tenacity to persevere. But I was confident because I believed that my outcome would be perfect even if it wasn't the outcome I thought I wanted. I trusted my Father's decision, but I made the choice to live and made my plea.

What I gave up was *trying*. I had to submit. To submit is "*to accept or yield to a superior force or to the authority or will of another person.*[9]" Submission requires humility. People often use the phrase "fight cancer." But there comes a point when fighting is not only futile but destructive. Fighting requires energy and attention; it is stress-inducing and often fear-driven. I chose to *yield* to my Father and rely on Him to save me. I prayed for every resource and opportunity to enter my path and manifest my healing. I was broken but, if I persevered, I would be built back up better than I otherwise would have been.

Humiliating things about hospital life

There is absolutely no pride in illness, believe me.

1. Male nurses

No matter how sick you are, you don't want a dude wiping you. Period. My male nurse thought he had his technique down. He used his hand like an ax. Very efficient. Very uncomfortable. Very embarrassing. I did not know that I could ask for another nurse.

2. Urination stimulus

You can use your imagination but never in life will you feel more like a piece of meat.

3. Weird poop

Those meds have to come out, eventually. And frequently!

4. No privacy when bathing

You don't get a locked door. The CNA comes in, they draw the curtain and you pray to God that nobody with bad manners decides to just barge in. Doctors sometimes stick their head in to ask a question and you run the risk of being exposed to the hallway behind them. I had a male CNA early on, who honestly did seem like he was getting mildly flirtatious as he bathed me because I happened to tell him he looked just like a friend of mine. I was only being friendly. It's an awkward situation. But even worse was that the head nurse, another guy, kept popping his head in to ask if everything was okay. I felt like the guy might be a felon or something and I wondered why he was there if they thought he was untrustworthy.

5. Measuring pee

#thatisall.

6. Morning rotations

Because they barge in on a girl before she's even had a chance to get her face together. You look like utter crap, boobs hanging all kinds of ways under a droopy hospital gown. Terrible. You have drool on your face, probably. Your breath stinks especially because you can never brush your teeth; it is too painful against gums, your wrists hurt and you can't hold a toothbrush. Besides, the brushes they give you don't clean your teeth, anyway.

7. Judgmental hospital workers.

This one is pretty hard. You expect your nurse to be supportive and helpful to a fault, given your obvious condition. This is what they went to school for. But not everyone is meant to take care of people. I could tell my male nurse was a jock. I could also tell he thought I wasn't trying hard enough. My suspicion was confirmed one day. In the early days, I didn't eat much, but it wasn't because of a lack of appetite or the anorexia I was later diagnosed with. It was because I couldn't handle utensils. Putting pressure on my wrists was impossible, made worse by the position of the table over my bed which was too high and required a sharper angle. So, I just wouldn't eat much. On this day, my rheumatologist's intern (I believe) came in for her weekly visit. She brought me a piece of chocolate. There was a full plate of food in front of me. I think she knew I couldn't manage. She asked if I needed help. I told her I couldn't cut the food because my wrists hurt. She encouraged me to ask for help. She told me not to be afraid to do so when I need it because that's what they're there for. Then she pushed the call button for the nurse. And WALKED. OUT. She just left me there to deal with Mr. Soccer Coach by myself. He asked what I needed and I asked him if he could cut my food for me. Honestly, it was one of the more pathetic things I've ever had to do. I felt bad asking and he immediately made me feel worse. He said something about seeing "a lot of people become deconditioned" in intensive care. NO SHIT GENIUS! Apparently, Mr. Universe didn't think I was trying hard enough and I was playing the victim. But who in their right mind asks a stranger to cut their food if it's not entirely necessary?

When everyone is basically expecting you to die

I'm a survivor
I'm not gon' give up
I'm not gon' stop
I'm gon' work harder
I'm a survivor
I'm gonna make it
I will survive

Keep on survivin'!
Destiny's Child, *Survivor*

It is a peculiar feeling when, in moments of brief lucidity, you are fully aware that everyone around you is just waiting for the clock to run out on your life.

In the ICU it's called "Sunset." During one of several dreadful stays there – breathing tube controlling the flow of air into and out of my body and preventing me from being able to cough on my own, feeding tube keeping me nourished, colostomy bag collecting my waste, and air compression bags inducing regular blood flow around my lower legs, connected to machines like a marionette – the only room I could see completely from my bed had a picture of a setting sun on an orange background with the word "SUNSET" printed in big black letters. I could see the elderly patient lying in bed and family members coming to say their final farewell. This was the only view I had. Not the most encouraging thing to see right after you go into an emotional meltdown because the doctor told you they would have to re-insert the feeding tube you had already successfully negotiated with your oncologist to have removed for mercy's sake, even though you were still not eating enough on your own and considered anorexic. Or when your little brother has to sign the authorization to have some tube thing inserted through the side of your neck to monitor something or other. It would be helpful to, at least, be able to see the real sun shining in the sky at times like that, I can assure you.

It becomes very clear what the people around you are thinking by the words they choose and their expressions. One of my doctors – the one who had told me the x-ray looked like a bomb had gone off in my chest – had a cute little habit that got the message across clearly. Every miserable morning, when she walked in for rounds, she would say, with what came across as suppressed disbelief, "You're such a trooper!" That confused me. Like, what else was I supposed to do? It didn't quite feel like the positive sentiment that she must have meant it to be but, then, I didn't see what she saw every day either. It seemed like she was expecting to see the inevitable empty bed. I interpreted "You're such a trooper" as, 'Wait, you're still here?' I smiled inside. I drowned out the thought by singing to myself that classic chorus from Beyonce's *Irreplaceable*:

> *You must not know 'bout me*
> *You must not know 'bout meeeeeeee*

I'm a survivor. I'm gonna make it. You really don't know me. My body wants to give up but my spirit won't let it. You know nothing about me. You know nothing.

Christmas Eve 2018, I was sitting at the dining room table with my mom. We were going to have a mini family reunion because two of my uncles and their families were coming. My mom looked up at me across the cluttered table. I don't remember her exact words but she recalled six years before, sitting in that very chair picking hymns for my funeral. One of my uncles has told me at least three times, "I gave up on you. Twice!" Another had asked if he should fly up to say goodbye.

Why me?

The chaplain would come to the oncology floor every once in a while. A very nice lady. I could tell that, even though she identified as Christian, she was there for the spiritual support of people of all beliefs. One day she asked the inevitable question, "Do you wonder 'why me'?"

I had thought about people asking that question before, when something bad happens to them. (My mind had time to wander, after all.) Like, "what did I do to deserve this?" In my mind, that question always had the implication that there was someone out there who would have actually deserved that person's fate. But my thinking was, "Why *not* me?" I'm just another person. Why would somebody else be more deserving of suffering than I was?

And what if I had to go through this to get to something better, to teach somebody something that will help them… or something?

My truth was that I was grateful for the opportunity. I was never promised that nothing bad would happen to me, but I was promised by God that He would be with me through every trial, disappointment, and suffering. The only things I had control over were my faith and my mind (in lucid moments, at least). Maybe it was the meds – and I know this will sound crazy – but I felt like I had been given a responsibility, that I had to carry this burden for someone who couldn't handle it. I was grateful for being given the strength it took to get through it. I was grateful for the blood of Jesus and I prayed for healing in His name. I was thankful for God's answer, even if it wasn't the answer I was looking for. On one of Pastor Clark's visits to me at home, we talked about praying for healing. I tearfully said, "But the answer could be no," as I reflected on the possibility of leaving my family, not getting the chance to have a family of my own, and not having a feeling that I had accomplished my purpose in life.

I did not say any of that, however. I sheepishly replied something about how it would be understandable for a person to think that but I didn't.

When everyone is basically expecting you to die, or when you are wholly reliant on others for your care, you learn a lot about people and relationships. When the storm passes you see the whole world differently.

The breakthrough

I think that, when people talk about miraculous healing in the context of faith, skeptics hear a mystical fairytale. Hocus Pocus. David Blaine and David Copperfield. But faith is very practical. I prayed for the things I needed to be healed, including the creativity, passion, brilliance, and commitment of my doctors to keep trying to figure something out. Because my situation was not a cookie-cutter one, it was very difficult; I didn't want them to give up on me. I had no doubt they were committed, I just wanted them to keep their momentum because I was desperately holding on for my breakthrough and I feared growing too weary to hold my grip.

And another rung in my climb out of the pit would always appear in the nick of time.

For example, I went into a brief remission from the Hodgkin disease. When it was discovered to have returned, chemo was out of the question because it exacerbated my scleroderma symptoms – so much so that I never got all four of the drugs that make up the ABVD regimen. I couldn't go back to that. Dr. Tsai began searching for other options. At just the right time, he found an immune therapy study at Sloane Kettering and my history with Hodgkin lymphoma perfectly matched the minimal requirements for consideration. The study was based on several DNA profiles from what I will call the "baseline patients," those whose DNA formed the basis of the treatment. To be included in the study a cheek swab was taken to get my DNA to find out if I had at least a 50% match to one of those profiles. After about two weeks, I found out there was a match! About a month after Dr. Tsai first told us about the study, my mom and I were headed to New York to begin treatment and I had a new oncologist.

One of the things that helped me to keep holding on was a prior autologous stem cell transplant, which cancer made me "lucky" to be able to receive. It is used as a treatment for scleroderma but only in the most extreme circumstances. I was also fortunate that the cancer had not spread to my bone marrow so my stem cells were "clean."

Immune therapy ultimately healed me. But I had to hold on to my faith long enough to get to that point – a circumstance I could never have anticipated – or I would have missed the opportunity to have my prayers answered.

That is how my life was saved. Every resource necessary for my miracle appeared at the exact moment it was needed.

CHAPTER NINE

Mind Over Matter

Note to self: Don't believe your circumstances

The day finally came when I really was being released from the hospital. Week after week, it was like a game of Chicken, being told I would be released "soon" but not being well enough to leave when the time came. Then, there was trouble finding a place that could take me. I'll get to that in a bit. Over and over, freedom would seem imminent, only to leave me disappointed.

Throughout the ordeal, I had to maintain my sanity and good spirits. I gave myself things to look forward to. One thing I was determined to do was to go to Miami. I would envision the white sandy beach, the blue sky, the crystal blue ocean... I wanted to be sexy and have fun under the warm sun. Miami was always on my mind. It was something to reach for. One day, my uncle called and, at some point during our talk, he mentioned that I should go to Miami once I got out. I had received confirmation! I couldn't believe he'd said that! I knew it was going to happen. In fact, soon after I was finally free, my mom treated me to the trip I had been dreaming about.

I found ways to entertain myself. I asked my mom to bring my *Whoopsie* doll. She had bought it for me when I was little. It's a hard brown doll with pigtails that shoot up and she lets out a high-pitched squeak when her stomach is pressed. I had fashion shows with my *Whoopsie* doll on the large windowsill in my hospital room. She had two outfits. I took pictures.

I love taking pictures with my cell phone. In my next life, I'll be a photographer. But in this life, I always take pictures when I am able to. I was fascinated by a large tree standing diagonally across from my room. It was late November, and this tree had the brightest orange and yellow leaves. It was beautiful. I took pictures of it. I even made a video about it. It felt like it was there for me because I, for one, would not have expected a tree to be so vibrant and full in late fall. The other trees were barren. I was told that it was of Chinese origin. But no matter, it was there as a reminder that there were light and hope, even in that dark place.

It was very important, to me, to be polite. It made me happy to be able to exude happiness, patience, and gratitude. I was grateful to everybody. I felt so fortunate to be where I was, to have access to that level of care, and that I didn't have to travel more than twenty-five minutes to get to it. Although, at that time, home seemed so far away. The thoracotomy left me with a hole in my back through which a long tube was extended into my lung. At the other end, the tube was attached to a "wound vac" that continuously sucked out excess fluid and puss to prevent infection. The tube was held in place by being stitched into my skin. I'm not sure how long it took me to figure out it was there, or that the container at the end of the bed wasn't for urine that I didn't realize I was releasing, but for the fluid coming out of my lung. It was always full of yellowish fluid. A large adhesive dressing covered the place where the tube was attached to my flesh and it had to be replaced so the wound could be cleaned every few days. It was a nightmarish experience every time, particularly because most of the nurses had no experience with it and often had to call a – usually annoyed – nurse from another floor to help. The skin in that area was extremely sensitive and every replacement of the dressing prevented the irritation from getting better. It required the nurse's patience but also the ability to work fast to minimize exposure. One night, a nurse who hadn't worked with me much had to do it. The IV machine I was always attached to would beep randomly when too many air bubbles were in the tube. It started to beep while she was trying to follow the instructions she was given. Meanwhile, I was squirming, whining, and – I think – also trying to give her some pointers. I remember having to get my will power together to get through it and sometimes I would have to ask them to stop because it was too painful and exhausting. At some point, this nurse began to get very agitated. And, in my emotional state, I began to cry. I was NEVER a crier. But I really cried like a baby at the thought of her being mad at me. I felt that, even though I was trying my best, people would still get mad. She asked me why I was crying. I babbled something about it. But then she said the most remarkable thing as she tried to explain that her frustration had nothing to do with me: she said, "Everybody says you're the nicest patient!"

From the pot to the fire to the pot again

I was very happy to finally be discharged from the hospital. But I wasn't out of the woods by any means. I had spent six months either lying down or sitting for about 99% of the time. My body had become severely deconditioned, as my not-so-empathetic male nurse had warned me it would. I would not be going straight home, but to a nursing home to be rehabilitated for a month. It made me happy to know that the place was only ten minutes away from home. Once again, I'd be spending my days hanging with the geriatrics. And today I know that no matter what, I will NEVER put my parent in a nursing home. There's something in the constitution about cruel and unusual punishment. It would probably be anti-American.

In the nursing home, I was very fortunate to have a large single room with a big window that looked onto what we'll claim as a courtyard. Unlike most of the seniors who occupied the building, I had many visitors. One of my favorite visitors was Pastor Clark. She'd come and pray with me and bring me food. One time, she asked what I would like her to bring and I asked for guacamole. She went to Whole Foods and got me guac and chips. My friend, Tiffany, came to visit from New York. This was her second visit; the first had been during another hospital stay. Other than Tiffany, only one friend visited me. I feel bad for Stan. A friend from high school, my mental fog overcame me and I couldn't keep myself "awake" to talk to him. But he brought me a rose. I don't even know how he knew I was there. My younger brother never came there, but he hadn't visited much even when I was in the hospital, and I was relieved that he didn't. He's the one person I would really rather have not seen me "dying." And it was hard to try to seem stronger than I was whenever he did visit. Now at ManorCare – the only place that would have me, despite a really nice nurse having warned me not to go – I was still visited by my church family. My mom still visited daily and it would always depress me if she had to skip a day.

A strange thing began to happen to me. I started aggressively scratching my skin. It felt like ants were crawling around underneath. It was anxiety. I just wanted to go home, I didn't want to be sick anymore, I just wanted to be free and happy. It is ironic that I had been "itching" to get out of the hospital and now that I was out, I was literally itching to go back. The nursing home, in a lot of ways, was far worse than the hospital. I ended up staying there only two of the four weeks I was scheduled to. I was constantly septic due to having basically no immune system while several areas of my body like my arm with the IV and my back with the wound vac, provided easy access for bacteria. I contracted pneumonia, which I think was, partially, because the nurse that came in to change the dressing around the IV did not create the sterile barrier required and even talked over me without a face mask. One morning, another nurse brought in a chair to sit in to check my weight, but it smelled like someone had had a diarrhea accident in it. I was genuinely elated to be back at HUP – it was like going from the wild jungle back to civilization.

PART THREE

Becoming

CHAPTER TEN

Melissa 2.0

Aftermath

February 21, 2016

It is still very difficult to talk about. I can think about it to myself, but when I speak about it out loud, or when someone else brings it up, it will cause me to fall to pieces. I am strong. I am resilient. I am highly pragmatic. I am very self-aware. I'm not a cry-baby or one to play the victim. But this will stop me in my tracks.

I will get to my therapist's office feeling confident and almost silly for being there. On my way up the elevator to the second floor, it feels like an obligatory exercise since I made the appointment and it's too late to cancel because it would be rude and I would still have to pay for the session. I pick up the phone in the hallway, punch in the code and let the person who answers know I am waiting at the door. They let me in and I take a seat in the waiting area of the architectural firm where the counseling office is. "What in the world is there to talk about?" I think to myself. My therapist comes out to greet me and I follow him to the office. I sit on the little couch across from his chair in the dimly lit room, and we chat for a while, going over the events of my life between appointments. He asks me what I would like to talk about today. I pick something. I may be annoyed about something that happened in a friendship or at church, the frustrations of trying to start a business. And we go from there. He writes notes in the notebook on his clipboard. But at some point, the conversation comes to the issue of grief. My grief. Up until that moment, I can speak rationally, bounce around ideas in my head... But we always end up getting to this place, where everything shuts down and I am at a loss for words. I feel vulnerable and exposed and uncomfortable and resistant to moving forward.

Even in the midst of misery, I did not allow myself to pity myself or feel defeated. By the time I was diagnosed with stage IV-B Hodgkin's lymphoma in March 2012, I had already been living with scleroderma for six years, and lupus for three. I had already suffered from some of the most debilitating symptoms of mixed connective tissue disease. I had already been living with an illness that was destroying my life and my body, even without cancer.

It's funny how you can feel about things *after* you've already been through them. In the moment, all that matters is surviving, getting through the ordeal by any means necessary. One day at a time. One moment at a time. One moment at a time. One moment at a time. Now, when I look back, I think I grieve for the person I see in retrospect. That she survived is nothing short of a literal miracle. No one expected her to survive, even in one of the best hospitals in America. What she had to go through. The toll the previous ten years has had on her physically, professionally, socially, and emotionally. In 2016, able to function in an almost completely normal manner, I can focus on the activities involved in rebuilding my life. And that is a blessing. But I would never want to see anyone go through what she has.

The word "grief" is my trigger. No one else speaks that word to me. People ask how I'm feeling and I'll tell them I'm fine, or I have a headache, or a cold or something. But I never say, "To be honest, I've never dealt with my grief. I need to grieve for the person who went to the bowels of hell so that she could stand here today, able to talk to you, free from most of her previous limitations."

The reluctant surgeon

Given the state I was in, I was surprised that my surgeon spoke to me as though he was done with my case. I was still very ill in 2013. He seemed assured that everything would be fine from there on out, even though I still had a deep wound from the procedure and was constantly septic. Surgeons are not known for their bedside manner! Since he seemed intent for that to be our last appointment, I did not bother to reach out to him again when things seemed not to be getting better with my wound. One night, while lying on the couch in the living room, my back felt wet. There had been a big bump over my wound for a while. The wound vac was gone by then. I thought it was sweat from a hot flash, as chemo triggered premature menopause. I reached behind me instinctively to wipe some of it away. When I saw my hand, there was a heavy yellow fluid on it. I asked my mom to look. She said there was something white showing through the skin. We thought it was just flesh. After I had her take a few pictures with my phone and she looked at it again, she said it looked like bone. She said she should try to take it out. At that point, pus was gushing out of the wound profusely. After pressing a little, a long, pointy piece of bone emerged from the wound. Naturally, I called Dr. Tsai's office immediately. "*What ELSE is going to happen*?" I thought. I was so sick of feeling like a freak. I put the piece of bone in a small tin box. (I still have it...) I learned that the persistent infection in my lungs had caused the bone to deteriorate. I had to schedule another appointment with the reluctant surgeon.

I explained what had happened. I think I even showed him the bone so he could verify what it was. With surprise, he asked why I hadn't come to see him sooner! I don't think I answered him, out of shock at the pretense. I don't even remember the rest of the appointment.

Postlude

I was really just killing time. Department stores are good for that. It's always nice to look at pretty things as you wait for time to pass. When I was very sick and my mom was my best friend, home aid and provider, the mall was the go-to destination for me to be outside and live a little. "Me and the geriatrics" were the only people who would be walking aimlessly around a mall mid-day on a Tuesday. My mom worked at night. On an early Tuesday afternoon in the mall, you see a lot of walkers with tennis balls at the ends of the legs or plastic "skates" like I had that loudly screeched as they slid choppily on the floor. Or wheelchairs. I was always the youngest, pushed by my senior citizen mother. A reversal of fortune? But this time I was by myself, walking carefully but freely. I don't remember what I was waiting for during this visit to Suburban Square in Ardmore, but I ended up wandering into Macy's. I stopped by the jewelry counter directly in front of the entrances, perusing the long gold necklaces for a moment. Then I walked further in, toward my right where handbags were laid out on a table. I looked up to see a somewhat familiar face. I couldn't tell if she was someone I knew or just resembled someone I knew. Something about that face was so familiar. After a few moments, I realized that she looked just like my sister. I looked down at the bags again. The next time I looked up our eyes met and I nodded a silent hello, I think. She replied politely. But, as I began to walk past her, I realized who she was. I said, "Excuse me, do you work at HUP?"

She said, "Yes."

"I think you were my nurse. My CNA."

"Yes! Yes, I remember you. Look at you! You look so good. How have you been?"

"Good. Thank you. I remember you because you look just like my sister. And my mom loved your gold earrings."

"Oh," she chuckled. "Yes. I remember *we thought you were going to die.*"

Now, I believe the legal term for that is "spontaneous utterance" and it could be perceived as, at least, impolite. But I took it as the compliment she meant it to be. I cannot imagine her perspective. The last time she had seen me, I really was lying on a fine, squiggly line between life and death. She had seen me when I had been completely incapable of taking care of myself. She had heard the doctors and nurses talking. She had seen many others, I'm sure, never make it out of the cancer ward. She is probably very familiar with the look of impending human demise. From my perspective, it was an oddly wonderful confirmation of what I had experienced and what it meant.

Whenever I meet someone who hasn't seen me since those times, the look in their eye and the sound of their voice has already become recognizable as well: awe. My survival, my recovery from certain death, is a miracle. I'd like to think that when people who know what I've been through see me, they realize that all things are possible. And that is the message I am destined to share.

ABOUT THE AUTHOR

Melissa Mavour is the host of the Rainbow in Bloom YouTube channel, where she shares her experiences and other information about living and thriving with scleroderma. It is intended to provide encouragement for those still weathering their own storm. She also hosts the Rainbow in Bloom podcast where she discusses business and personal development.

Born in New York City, Melissa was raised by her mother and grandmother both in the U.S. and the Caribbean. She has earned a B.S. in Economics from Chestnut Hill College and an M.S. in International Transportation Management from SUNY Maritime College.

An entrepreneur at heart, she continues to work at building her transportation business. Melissa is happy to complete this book, a labor of love that she started several years ago when she began to recover from her illness.

Today, Melissa looks forward to seeing the world, falling in love, eating good food, and making new friends.

Sources:

1. https://www.medscape.com/viewarticle/761828
2. https://www.verywellhealth.com/drug-methotrexate-cancer-risk-3975004
3. https://medlineplus.gov/druginfo/meds/a682019.html
4. https://www.ncbi.nlm.nih.gov/pmc/articles/PMC2763717/
5. https://en.wikipedia.org/wiki/Anecdotal_evidence
6. https://tim.blog/guest/dr-andrew-weil/
7. https://www.lupus.org/resources/the-ana-test-for-drug-induced-lupus
8. http://www.script-o-rama.com/movie_scripts/h/the-house-bunny-script-transcript.html
9. https://www.google.com/search?rlz=1C5CHFA_enUS765US765&q=Dictionary#dobs=submit

Made in the USA
Columbia, SC
23 January 2021